THE RIDICULOUS

Adventures of Adventurers

BOOK 1

A Novel

JEFFREY NEIL KIPPEL &
MINDY HEATHER BLACKSTIEN

Copyright © 1986, 2018, 2020, 2021, 2022, 2023
JEFFREY NEIL KIPPEL
& MINDY HEATHER BLACKSTIEN
THE RIDICULOUS
Adventures of Adventurers
BOOK 1
A Novel
All rights reserved.

No part of this publication may be reproduced, distributed, or transmitted in any form or by any means, including photocopying, recording, or other electronic or mechanical methods, without the prior written permission of the publisher, except in the case of brief quotations embodied in critical reviews and certain other non-commercial uses permitted by copyright law.

JEFFREY NEIL KIPPEL
& MINDY HEATHER BLACKSTIEN

Printed Worldwide
First Printing 1986
First Edition 1986
Eighth Printing 2023
Eighth Edition 2023

17 16 15 14 13 12 11 10 9 8

This book is a work of fiction. Any references to historical events, real people, or real places, products and services are used fictitiously. Other names, characters, places and events are products of the author's imagination, and any resemblances to actual events, products, things, places or persons, living or dead, is entirely coincidental.

For information, interviews, media bookings and copies, visit:
www.RidiculousNovels.com

Amazon recognized *The Ridiculous* as a #1 read across vast categories spanning Comedy to Happiness to Science Fiction to Self-Help & Psychology Humor.

Meet a being whose soul unexpectedly finds residence in the fuzzy bodysuit of an alien somewhere in outer space. With a practical, joke loving AI-infused intergalactic ship as his travel companion, things go from ridiculous to RIDICULOUS.

Moreover, the human's birth body becomes a vessel for the extraterrestrial—who actually seems quite content. He had known of Earth, never been, so he was ready to explore.

(That, and he was on the run.)

Join a cast of outlandish personalities as they embark on a thrilling journey filled with ridiculous antics, surreal meet-ups, out-of-this-world snackventures, and random wonderings that are sure to make you go "hmm."

Set against the backdrop of sci-fi fantasy, comedy and satire, The Ridiculous may surprise you. Beyond humor, it possesses heart.

(Just ask the characters.)

Want More RIDICULOUS? If you find The Ridiculous made you laugh out loud, rethink your thoughts, or take new good-for-me action, you can earn RIDICULOUS rewards. So, get creative, tell your stories, share your "aha's" and tag #DoRidiculous #DoRi

www.DoRidiculous.com

The International Review of Books

General Summary for Context

"We hop onboard this riotous journey with Serbinand and his little buddies as they navigate the experiences of their imagination.

These amazing experiences can involve anything from being on a beach to savoring the newness and taste of food, and they can be anywhere from a ship to a gastro pub. They chat, argue, and enjoy all the events that come their way with a childlike intensity and joy that is both funny and exciting.

General Thoughts on the Novel

"I enjoyed it. While some novels require a great deal of analysis, thought and concentration, this one simply allows the reader to just be in the moment the way children are. It's so ridiculous it's a riot to read, but also at times gives us food for thought as to things in life we take for granted (taste, smell, touch, etc.) An excellent laugh-out-loud escape from reality. Highly recommended."

Supportive Critique

"Since this book is whatever you want it to be, I cannot fathom how anyone could find an 'error.'"

I Loved Every Freaking Second of It.

"An excellent, bizarre, intelligent and hilarious piece of work. I was talking about it after reading it. I'm still talking about it. My wife even heard me laughing and asked what was going on. I think this book is going to be a big hit. Very strong morals. There are even lessons that bring value. The writing was really strong. It is really good."

Michael Evan, Canada
Podcast Host & Literary Publicist Fantasy / Sci-Fi Focus, Founder

Better than Hitchhikers!

"I used to be a sci-fi buff when I was young. I followed the adventures of *Hitchhiker's Guide to the Galaxy* and always enjoyed it. Reading through *The Ridiculous: Adventures of Adventurers - Book 1*, I was reminded of it through the fun, adventurous, and zany journeys the authors took me on. They nail it with this story - it's adventurous, fun, surprising and I couldn't put it down!

"I highly recommend picking up The Ridiculous for a great trip away from your daily rituals, as it will take you away on a fun, futuristic, funny adventure…and back!"

Joel Mandelbaum, Canada
#1 Best Selling Author, Winning Online

This Book Is Not My Typical Genre to Read but I Loved It!

"It is very creative, zany and funny, and the characters are very engaging and likable. The writing is very accessible and funny - in fact, I had a continuous smile on my face and laughed out loud many times as I read this book! Beneath the jokes and lightheartedness are some wonderful messages of self-acceptance, self-love and found friendship. This is the first in a series and I can't wait for the next book! Very well done!"

Stephanie Wilson, Canada
Freelance Copy Editor

The Book Truly Blew My Mind

"I honestly believe your publication is going to be a MASSIVE success! Truly it is so unique and entertaining. It honestly brings me so much joy. This book is one that truly stands out to date."

Chris E, South Africa
Marketing Director
Sci-Fi Fantasy Cover Designer

A Must Read…And Read AGAIN!

"Fun. Full of action. My family and I are big fans. The crazy adventures and multilayered characters are perfect as a great escape of the ordinary."

AJ Quevedo, USA
Life Coach & Transformation Specialist

I Read the First Chapter of This Book on My Podcast Open Book.

"It was a delight! The authors excel in the playfully fun comedy genre. Though the basis was silly as it was meant to be, the descriptions of the various alien species made it feel like you could visualize the crazy, almost natural way the universe could become! 10/10 will read again!"

Kevin Johnson, USA
Podcast Host, Open Book

My Students Love It!

"My students are much impressed with your book and want to read it many times. Whenever they are coming to me they are recalling the Author Talk which we had with you. I am very, very thankful to you."

Dr. Chivani Jain, India
Indian International School, Librarian

Two Hilarious Thumbs Up!

"A fabulous read that's highly recommended and addictively page turning. Hilarious and creative twist of comedic sci-fi will have you anxiously awaiting the next supplement! Such an entertaining read from talented authors."

Daryl Gazey, Canada
Retired Police Officer & Fitness Guru

It Is What It Is…Ridiculous - but I Mean That in the Nicest Possible Way.

"The thing about Sci-Fi and Fantasy is that you are only limited to what your imagination can conjure up…then I would say that you have accomplished that 'anything goes' ideology successfully.

"Speaking as a sci-fi nut and 'enthusiast' of Classic British comedy, I gotta say I loved it. All the elements were there; Star Wars, Star Trek, Python, and of course, the one that set the tone - Hitchhikers!"

Alan Irving, UK
Narrator, The Ridiculous
Voice-over Artist

Needs to Be a Movie. Very funny!

"Superb audiobook, needs to be a movie, very funny! This book had me laughing for the amazing diversity in voice acting in the actors and constant ridiculousness slipped into the story.

"This is a lot like a Monty Python skit or Hitchhiker's Guide to the Galaxy. This book has pieces of wisdom mixed in with outrageous hubris and you can visualize the sci-fi adventure.

"The only way it could be better is if there was a movie to materialize the hilarious characters and funny interactions and clumsiness."

Audible Review, USA

I Really Enjoyed the Light-Hearted and Easy-Going Style of This Book.

"I had no way of predicting what would happen next, and the author's side-bar conversations with the audience and with the characters brought the whole story to light in a most unique and playful way!

"The unconventional sci-fi story also shares a warm narrative that each of us can apply to our own lives. On a deeper level, my takeaway is that this is a story about resilience, about managing through change, about embracing new ideas and perspectives on reality, and it's about looking into an individual's soul and heart as the real essence of a being.

"Serbinand and the band of characters in the book are future, present and past all at once – it's a fun way of looking at space, time and our universe!

"As an adult, I enjoyed relating to the references the author made to so many things we've all grown up with, but for the generations that follow mine there is just playfulness and a grounded connection to the imaginary family of characters created.

"For anyone looking for a silly and playful approach to life, pick up or listen to *The Ridiculous: Adventures of Adventurers - Book 1.*"

Lisa Meller, USA
Team USA Diving Coach
World Champion Competitive Diver

I'm a Big Fan of Simon Carr Books and This Is Just as Wacky, Laugh- Out-Loud, Fun and Downright Crazy!

"I might have to get it on audiobook now as that would be hilarious (though I'd need headphones for sure - just listened to the sample on here and it brought back so many laughs from the reading!).

"Lots of references and similarities to classic 80's sci-fi / comedy but there's definitely no book like this! Ridiculous, smile-inducing and a wonderful escape."

RK, United Kingdom

This Book Really Needs to Be a Movie

"Very talented voice actor who helps you keep track of characters. This book really needs to be a movie haha. The character Orville reminds me of Kevin from Final Space. There are some characters who are lovable and none of them are without faults which is perfect.

"The book knows what type of book it is trying to be and that allows for some side-splitting laughter.

"It's very rare to have a laugh from writing alone so my hat goes off to the writers. The made-up words used as if they are real is hilarious as you can still visualize what is happening."

Audible Review, United States

This Book Was Very Creative and Funny.

"My children and I all loved it. Can't wait for book 2. I also think it's great how he brought the story together with all the Author interruptions."

M. Rose, Canada

Laugh-Out-Loud Fun!

"Ridiculously fun story just as the title suggests! A big round of applause to the authors for taking on an adventure that I am excited to continue. And that says a lot since sci-fi is not my genre of choice normally.

"I can't wait for the next installment to come out. I finished this story in one sitting and sad that it was already over… for now.

"Since I originally wrote this review I have gone back to read again. Second time around was just as funny and the pick me up I needed."

Jennifer Asplet, USA

Magnificent Read!

"My family and I are big fans of The Ridiculous sci-fi adventure book. The crazy adventures to the multilayered characters are perfect for a great escape of the ordinary.

> Rosalie Dinkin, Canada
> Metaphysical Minister

Ok, This Book was…Ridiculous.

"Definitely not something I would have picked up with my own two hands, but I am SO glad it was recommended to me. It was the perfect change of pace from reading the more serious fiction I typically pick up.

"This is anything but serious. It's hilarious. Has the exact vibes as Hitchhiker's Guide to the Galaxy only with a singing bird thrown in. Not like a chirp-chirp singing bird, but a bird with opera enhanced vocals as its talking voice.

"I did have the pleasure of listening to this on Audible, which I am sure added to the hilarity. The narrator did a freakishly amazing job acting out the characters… including the author himself. Yes. The author shows up as a character in his own book. Because when you have a book about body-switching aliens and get stuck without knowing what's supposed to happen next… why not? 5 Stars for putting a smile on this reader's face."

> Amanda, USA

A Ridiculous Ride into The Universe…

"A sci-fi comedy starring Serbinand, a space nomad, and Godfried, his talking ship with an attitude. It is funny, irreverent, and ridiculous, just as the title suggests. It takes you into wild places of the author's imaginary universe. The author has a unique voice and speaks to you like your secret mischievous self. I look forward to reading it again on audio!"

> Y. Lam, USA

5.0 out of 5 stars. A Great Reading Adventure! Yes!

"This is a 5-star read for teens and adults alike! I am a huge fan of "The Ridiculous" and its authors, Jeff and Mindy! It's a different world, an exciting adventure, a funny story with laugh-out-loud moments as well as thought-provoking ideas with deeper meaning throughout! I love the made-up words, the beautiful names, and the description which sparks the imagination! I look forward to hearing the audible version too and can really see this as a sci-fi movie! Highly recommend!"

Susan Schwartz Educator
Author & Editor

Ridiculous, Hilarious, and Filled with Great Messages Reviewed in Canada on September 20, 2023

"The book certainly lives up to its name...it's truly a wonderful, hilarious journey and a joy to read. The authors have infused some self-help, care and wisdom along the way, anchoring the book with excellent food for thought (and food does factor prominently in this book, too:) Sit back, and enjoy the ride!"

Joey Gill
Media Relations Consultant & Publicist

Praise for the Audiobook: Truly an Amazing Experience!

"I decided that I would sit down, relax and immerse myself in The Ridiculous Audible. I knew this one was going to be different. My very pleasant surprise was how I was feeling listening to the book. It made me laugh out loud and feel good and it was so much fun listening to all the different voices of all the characters! I can't even imagine how difficult it was to get all the voices of the characters! And the story script is amazingly told. I would highly recommend this audiobook and will be listening to the story again and again! This was and is a great escape out of the ordinary! Great job to the author's Jeffrey Neil Kippel and Mindy Heather Blackstien! Also Alan Irving - I commend you on your great performance!"

Shoshana Diamond, Canada

TABLE OF CONTENTS

PART ONE 1
    THE EXPLORERS
CHAPTER ONE 3
    SREEFS & RHINOKICKERS
CHAPTER TWO 23
    BAKED BEANS & JIME
CHAPTER THREE 29
    *GODFRIED THE !@$!!!***&%@#!!!!!*
CHAPTER FOUR 41
    SO NOW WHAT, HUH JIME?
CHAPTER FIVE 55
    INTERMISSION
PART TWO 57
    THE EXCHANGE
CHAPTER SIX 59
    THE TRANSFER
CHAPTER SEVEN 63
    STRANGE BODIES
CHAPTER EIGHT 89
    REVELATIONS
CHAPTER NINE 103
    CHARACTERS WITHOUT AN AUTHOR
PART THREE 123
    A NEW ADVENTURE
CHAPTER TEN 125
    UNDERSTANDINGS
CHAPTER ELEVEN 139
    THE SHIP
CHAPTER TWELVE 159
    NEXT STEPS
CHAPTER THIRTEEN 177
    GODFRIED'S TURN
GET TO KNOW THE AUTHORS 199
    JEFFREY NEIL KIPPEL & MINDY HEATHER BLACKSTIEN
GRATITUDES 203

PART ONE

THE EXPLORERS

"The will to do springs from the knowledge that you can do."

~ James Allen

CHAPTER ONE

SREEFS & RHINOKICKERS

From the distant star of Placellner he traveled. Why? Who knows...But that's not the point. At least not right now. And actually, it wasn't a star. It was a planet...his. HALT. In fact, that actually is the point. Serbinand, the larger-than-life space traveler who was always easy-going (except for right now), just escaped (barely) from his father's dominion where he was about to get married to Anslow from Parduchina—or maybe buried is a better word. Anslow had this habit of burp-singing hysterically for five minutes and seven seconds, every three to eight hours. Who could put up with that? Sure, she had almost every cool toy and gadget Serbinand would ever want to play with, but if his heart wasn't feeling loved and loving, was it even worth it? After convincing the fortifiers that he was leaving momentarily just to get a sreef sandwich, or something better, he managed to find his ship, who had been patiently waiting for his immediate getaway (which actually took about 47 weeks and zero and a half days).

So, for three billion galactic years and nine point two mega seconds, his ship careened across the somewhat vast universe, turning left here and right there and looping around deltic spagnoids every so often. All in all, it was smoooooth trekking well, besides the mishap near the Algernon sector, ahem, which we won't get into right now.

His journey would have been a lot shorter had he not stopped in at *Joe's Galactic Bar*. But who could blame him? With all the advertising that Joe had been doing lately, he wouldn't be surprised if a Cornsharr actually did stop by. You know the slogan: "No party is complete without a Cornsharr. Why not stop in and try *Joe's Galactic Bar*!"

What the hayhorff is a Cornsharr?, the space traveler thought as he came within a safe distance of the place. (A Cornsharr is a mythical creature created out of the corn of pop. To communicate, it rubs its own belly. This generates the heat needed to pop more of its own corn. A single corn popping out of its corn-hole signifies "yep". Three popped corns signify "nope." And two, umm yeah, that's just a bum belch. Oh, and when the corns erupt into a rainbow of colors, well, that's when the party gets started. Let's just say "YUM". ~ Letting ya know in case ya were not yet aware. Signed, the Author.) Anyway, he decided why not and stepped in for several sreefs and a shot of his favorite drink, the Rhinokicker. This strange and bizarre sort of alcoholic substance got its name during the Age of Bartenders. It is much like one of the Olden Age soft drinks called Briozza, which was banned under section 77.56 of the Living Rights Act supplement 999.887.172.31457-Q. Unlike Briozza though, it's claimed that 3.289 seconds after tasting the Rhinokicker, one would kick back their legs in a sort of dance and charge something, sometimes even a brick wall, scream-singing "rhino, rhino, rhino!" Apparently, the drink was smokin'! The Rhinokicker has no such effect on Serbinand, although he has claimed to have hallucinated packs of rhinos kicking out dance moves around his head. It was quite the delight, actually.

With drink in hand, Serbinand was now able to sit back for a moment. Finally free to get acquainted with his beverage, he wanted to get in touch with his feelings, or at least try. He'd been through a lot these last few hours, hmmm, these last few weeks, no—months, no—years, no—ummm, uhhhh…actually, to be safe, these last few decades. Now is the time to set things straight, he decided, or at least attain some quasi-entertaining fashion of existence.

And if that didn't work…well, then he'd have to wreak havoc. Maybe even disrupt flight schedules just to get everyone to experience airport food on a continuous loop across all known galaxies. And then, to really confuse people, maybe he'd get all planes flying to the same destination - one giant lovefest. Actually, one giant lovefest where the only law is to love yourself. (Wow, that would be nice.) Or maybe he'd just brush his teeth. Decisions, decisions. Hmmm while each scenario is fulfilling in various ways, only one would leave him with that tingly mouth feel. Ahhh.

"Where yaoftta?" asked some *thing* sitting on the bar stool above him.

Serbinand wanted to answer the fuzzy creature, but he couldn't find its head anywhere. He didn't want to embarrass it by speaking to the wrong part of its body, so he just ignored it.

"Have ya been drinkin' the Deafbonker, or are ya just ignorin' me?" it asked, slightly annoyed.

The voice appeared to be coming from the *thing's* foot. So going on speculation, Serbinand spoke to its foot.

"Sorry...I...Ummm...I didn't hear you. Actually, I thought I heard a pack of dancing rhinos coming this way, so I got scared and turned off my hearing senses." Serbinand was quite pleased with this ingenious story, especially the part about turning off his hearing senses (as if he really could do that with any degree of accuracy).

Serbinand hoped that his words were enough to turn this creature off and make it go away. But he had no such luck. It just sat there...as if assessing the situation, trying to figure out the best possible course of action. This seemed to be going on for close to an eternity. Then, right when Serbinand thought enough time had passed and he could turn away, it spoke.

"Oh...I see ya been drinkin' the Rhinokicker. Never liked the drink m'self. Used to wake up with bumps on top of bumps on top of bumps, and brick shavings lodged into m' forehead... which, of course, made it very painful to walk."

After that short but meaningful exchange of words both speakers decided it would be in their best interest to disregard the conversation and pretend it never existed. And with that, Serbinand casually glanced around the room, trying not to make eye contact with anyone or any *thing* else. You never know what that could lead to, especially since Cornsharrs may party here. *What the hayhorff is a Cornsharr?* he pondered again while scratching his head and contorting his face.

Directly in front of him sat this large brass contraption that looked like it made Carpacicino or Esmerato or some other kind of exotic, mega-money-loving coffee. Y'know the kind that is so strong that a teeny tiny cup is necessary just to ensure you don't overdrink. As if that would happen anyway. I mean, the liquid practically

~ 6 ~

solidifies on contact, leaving a black ultra mega sticky film around the rim…and your lips (if you don't lick 'em quick enough, that is).

Off to either side of the brass machine stood a huge assortment of glasses. Small ones, tall ones, square ones…. There were even those yellow flat ones. Yep, flat glasses…genius!

Above the counter in an elaborate rack sat different liquors. An alcohol lover's dream, and a Magic Show all in one. There were drinks of every possible color that one could think of, and more. Floating in the air, somehow, was an array of smoking funnels. They collected liquids from various beverage bottles which then poured into multiple little tubes. This is where the drink deliciousness was actually created. It mixed reds and greens, purples and yellows, and lighter yellows too, blending them all together to create a masterpiece sparkling with grandeur. The little tubes then emptied their contents into a spot over the counter where the glasses anxiously awaited (except the yellow flat ones). This visual effect was further enhanced by a blinking show of spiraling lights washing over the entire contraption. Seeing the wave of liquids float through the maze inspired Serbinand to order yet another drink just to watch the whole process again. Mid-thought, Serbinand noticed a golden goblet labeled "voice-box". It hung in the air. *Ah, a box that needs a voice. I have a voice,* Serbinand realized. *I should tell this box that I'll order another.*

"Hey, I'll order another," Serbinand yelled to the goblet.

"You'll wait fer yer bartender to take yer order first," it barked.

Serbinand, taken aback, quickly aborted that mission and tried to play it cool. It worked, for a moment. Glancing to his right an odd array of plant-like fauna caught his attention. He gasped and shook his head to stare wide-eyed. They were HUGE…Some even had spotted leaves or something that "simulated" leaves. Others were off-green and appeared to be quite normal. And then there was that red one next to the orange one which rested near itself…Oh, wait…that's a mirror. Mirror aside, Serbinand became very curious about these plants. So curious, in fact, that he jumped out of his seat and bolted into the garden area, hand already stretched out ready to feel if they were truly real.

"One inch lower and I'll rip your arm out of its socket and use it as a flyswatter!" blurted out a yellow one that Serbinand hadn't even noticed before.

Sorry, I didn't…mean to…uh…upset you. Hmm…are you a plant? Uhh, yeahhh, no you wouldn't be a plant, you talk…"

"I am a plant. That's a plant. And that's a plant too. We are all plants," it stated while looking around erratically (*possibly to find a fly that needed swatting*, Serbinand reasoned). "Do you have some sort of issue with plants? Or more specifically with the *Planta Intelligentisia* variety that we have become!

Hearing this, Serbinand couldn't help but be somewhat intrigued. Of course, he'd heard of *Planta Intelligentisia* before. In fact, he had recently planted some of their seeds on his ship, but those hadn't even sprouted yet. So, yes, Serbinand was amazed to finally be in the same room with so many of them and smiled wide.

Their leaf leader did not seem to care however, and continued, "Do you not realize how amazing we really are?" (He did.) "How long it took us to develop speech?" (That he was unsure about).

"How many thousands of years we had to listen to creatures like you spew words at us until we figured it out?" (Again, he was stumped...numbers weren't his thing. No worries though because an answer was not what the pompous plant was wanting. Rather it wanted to continue to be pompous, and that's precisely what played out). "How's my little planty doing today?", it mocked. "Would mama's doll like some more water?", "How about a little sing-songy song," he, it, they, or whatever continued, "You are my sunshine, my only sunshine," it sang. "Ahhhhhhh! Sure, it helped us grow faster. Sure, it helped us become the advanced and highly intelligent beings we are today, but come on...Why the high-pitched squeaky voices, the spittles of spit and the morning breath, oh my gosh...the morning breath! Y'all got to get a handle on that. Feed yourselves better, will ya, and then you'll stop pooping in your pelvis!" Serbinand didn't quite understand that part, but since it was *Planta Intelligentisia* speaking, he knew it must somehow make sense.

"Listen, I am truly sorry. I didn't know. If it is alright with you, I'll just leave y'all alone and get back to my drink or something." Serbinand spurted out.

"Wait, wait ...I was having fun showing off. Please stay," it seemed to apologize. Serbinand would have reconsidered had it not continued to show off, but it did. "...because we earned the bragging rights, you know. Our species did master evolution and all. That's why we need to spread our wisdom far and wide, a and—"

"That's ok, my ship is pretty narrow in the spots where it's not wide," Serbinand interrupted, "so I don't think I'd be a help anyway. In fact, I'm quite content to just go on my way. It was nice meeting you." And with that, he dashed off, grateful for the Rhinokicker drinkers whose raucous drowned out the plant's pleas to stay.

Wow, that was whacked, Serbinand thought, *although it was interesting, I must say.*

Serbinand returned to his barstool. After successfully placing his order for sreefs and granknuts, he decided to look around again. But this time to his left (the bartender's right). And that's when he saw her. Oh, she was beautiful - well, for a Draknoid. She was actually glowing! And what a large, hulking hunk standing right there beside her…albeit, grimacing at everyone and everything. It looked like he could probably topple someone over just by breathing in their direction (morning breath or not). At that moment Serbinand felt motivated to disregard the golden goblet "for bartenders only rule" completely, and almost shouted "mouthwash stat". Fortunately, his mind urged him to hold back, and instead reminded him that he could actually turn into his own hulking hunk. He pondered that for a moment and realized that going to the gym to pick things up and put them down (again and again and again) would truly be more exciting than doing nothing at all. At least his attention would be self-focused. But for now, he opted to do nothing at all and just continued to stare.

Beyond the *beauty and her hunk* was a pyramid-shaped dance floor. There were beings—or things—moving around in strange patterns. Dancing, likely. Serbinand never liked dancing. At least that's what he thought. The truth is he lacked confidence. Not that that was his fault. Someone, somehow, somewhere, at some time in his life must have said or done some*thing* that triggered his subconscious mind to create a dysfunctional Belief System—also known as B.S. Yes, B.S. that made him believe he was not a good dancer and could never be one. It was a needless belief that he was not even aware he had adopted. Yet he unknowingly allowed it to influence his entire sense of self-worth and as a result omitted what could have been one of his life's greatest joys. How crazy is that!?

Serbinand actually remembered many times hanging out at parties talking to others who felt similar and also chose not to dance. Each of them would rattle off all kinds of reasons—that seemed sound and logical—as to why it was better to stand back and only watch the action. *Clearly, though, the dancers were having more fun,* Serbinand reflected. They definitely were smiling more, seemed blissfully energized, and were even gifting their body with bountiful benefits. With that, Serbinand decided then and there that should a dance floor open up under his feet, in the future, he would dance. Well, once he learned how to coordinate his hands and feet, he thought. *Are your hands open? Closed? By your side? Up in the air? And what if you have an itch? How do you scratch an itch while still moving to the music?!* Serbinand felt himself getting anxious, thwarted once again by his subconscious mind into "believing" that to enjoy dancing you need to look, act or move in a certain way, rather than just feel the music. *I wish the plants had given me a lesson on dancing too,* Serbinand secretly thought.

At that point, his stomach rumbled so loudly that his body shook. It may even have looked like he was dancing, he thought with a giggle. So, he decided to return to one of his favorite thoughts–food! He glanced around for the menu, and saw it in the form of a sign:

Joe's Exotic Foods

You name it, we'll cook it…as long as it's legal!

We serve anything from ashiowerkat to zafelnuggs.

We can spice it with any spice, even if it's more than one!

So, don't be shy. Ask your server

— or anyone who looks like they work here —

and we'll be happy to grant your every request!

(Relating To Food Only.)

Pretty straightforward, Serbinand thought. He was so hungry though that he felt he didn't have the time, desire nor patience to visualize each type of food he'd ever liked, wanted to try or dreamt about repeatedly. So, he ordered one of his usuals. While waiting, and with not much else to do but think, he began salivating over the exotic dishes his mind conjured up anyway. (Some things you just can't control.) Mid-drool, the bartender greeted him with a toothless smile and his food. Actually, it was a one-tooth smile, and the sreefs were burnt.

As Serbinand was about to start eating, that thing that annoyed him earlier decided now was the perfect time to speak again–obviously concluding that enough time had passed since their last exchange of words. Wrong.

"So, where'ryaoffta anyways?" it asked.

"What makes you think I am going somewhere?"

"Well, there's a large arrow drawn on the front of your shirt which says, *this way or where else*, and on the back it says, *I'm going on vacation, anywhere besides here, so don't ask me about my tax returns because I am going away. Definitely somewhere.* So obviously I assumed you were going somewhere."

"Well, that's silly to assume" Serbinand slurred in between gulps of food, "cuz when you assu—"

"Yea, I know, when you assume you make an ass out of *u* and *me*."

Serbinand was hoping to derive some sort of satisfaction by telling that classic line and now felt extremely depressed that this fuzzy green creature spoiled that for him too. Serbinand had no interest in speaking to it any further and returned to his dinner.

"So, ...Ya come here often?"

Again! What did he have to do to make it stop?

"No." *Maybe short answers will give him the hint,* Serbinand thought. "Talkative tonight, aren't we?" it laughed.

"Listen, whatever and whoever you are, or are trying to be, I've had a rather hectic few weeks. Sure, I'm now free, or so it seems, but there was just so much confusion. Something about a missing blueraw pie—so we were shouted at, shot at, and then told very sternly to return home. That was by far the worst, and yet I still somehow managed to escape Placellner. My computer and I of course knew about this getaway months ago," Serbinand reflected while shaking his head, "but neither of us ever thought about what to do once we got out. So, we just circled and circled some strange galaxy over and over and over again and again and again."

In the midst of the 38th circle, we accidentally caused a small intergalactic skirmish or something, and just barely escaped with the ship intact. That is until we hit a freak asteroid downpour head on. This caused a major problem with the internal circuits and turned my flamboyantly fun friend Godfried into the most boastful super annoying, selfish and aggravating-to-me entity possible, also known as my ship's computer.

Now, not only do we have my father and his counsel, and Anslow and her people after us, it seems we started a parade of sorts. Multiple ships followed after us into the asteroid bath, perhaps hoping it led to a celebration with free gifts and flying plates of food. Having our own procession didn't help our anonymity much and instead attracted policing units from numerous star systems, all who decided that now was the best time to collect on every single type of ticket and splitsglitt that I, ummm, owed. And to top it all off I still have to cope with Godfried's new personality.

I tried to keep calm as best as I could under the circumstances, yet I only barely convinced Godfried not to stop, sign and smile for each ticket, and instead leave immediately. Miraculously, I succeeded after the first thirteen attempts. I then spent the next few hours trying to get the hot water to work so I could shower away all that happened. In the midst of trying, and still unshowered, I resolved to stop into some cool place to get something exciting to eat, quietly, minding my own business and not really talking to anyone so as not to arouse suspicion," Serbinand babbled, unaware he had just spoken.

That is, until he quickly realized he just did.

"Umm…hmmm…Oh Shazbot! I guess I, umm, just blew it all by telling you this here story. Yikes. So, umm, if you don't mind… I guess that leaves me with only two alternatives. Either I find a way of getting rid of you, or I get myself out of here quite quickly before you figure out what I've just said. And since I clearly am not (yet) a fan of picking heavy things up and putting them back down (again and again), I'm not quite equipped with the strength I need to get rid of you, umm, easily. And…being that I don't know what you're truly capable of, I think I better go. Buh-bye."

Serbinand jumped off his seat so suddenly that he knocked over three of those flat yellow glasses, launching particles of granknuts into the bar area. This set off an internal alarm that signaled the camera to take his photo, which he posed eloquently for. The alarm then alerted the guards to be on guard at all possible exits, including the way-off one to the right of the bar that no-one really knew about. All this commotion did nothing to help Serbinand keep a low profile. So, he decided he better get on with his escape.

"I'm comin' with you," the thing said. "No, you are *not*!"

"Yes, I am," it insisted.

"No way. Nope. No, you are *not*!" Serbinand insisted louder. "Well…"

"Well, nothing," Serbinand exclaimed as he started to run for the door, no longer pausing to look at it during the conversation. It worked. By the time fuzzy green lifted its foot to speak again Serbinand was gone. He was rid of that funky dunky being. However,

Serbinand didn't get too far. Two tiny beetle-like creatures carrying rather heavy artillery casually maneuvered him to the back of the very establishment from which he was trying to escape.

The three of them marched in unison down a maze of hallways toward a door laden with signs, such as:

~~and...~~

The Office:

Privacy must be maintained. (At all costs, or else.)

Thank you for your understanding – Have a nice day.

If you are reading this,

you are standing way too close.

So, GO AWAY!

It is time to leave.

Blessed BE thee.

There were others, but the words *'go away'* seemed to catch Serbinand's attention. So, he turned to *go away*. At that moment the door swung open. Before he could think *"whoaaa"*, he was ushered into a hard-wooden chair and told to wait for further instructions.

The room was neither small nor large. It was just *there*, well *here* (here for Serbinand, that is...but you're not Serbinand, so, yeah...Hmm...let's just say the room existed). It had no decorations other than balloons, streamers, tables of scientific dream jars and snow-filled pickle tubes. With no windows, there was really no light in the chamber, except for a few rays of sun that made their way in through a gap in the wall. Directly in front of Serbinand was an executive desk, mahogany. It was littered with papers, a partially eaten feast, two and a half keys, a nebulizer, a belly button tool and four dust nuggets. The beetles had taken their place on either side of the desk. One started eating the partially eaten feast, which smelled pretty good. Behind the pulpit was another door. It was made of steel, had a brass outline and looked official, really official.

It contained only one official sign:

Official Entry Only.
The Official Place Where ALL Official Errors Are Dealt With…Officially.

Ahh, looks like I've come to the right place, he thought enthusiastically. "Ahh…er…excuse me, but I think that you've made a slight err…" Serbinand started….

This whole situation reminded him of his youth when he was called into the Headmaster's office to defend some sort of incident he was only partially aware he had started. That resulted in all sorts of kerfuffles. Serbinand chuckled at the memory.

"Shhhhhhhhhhhhhhhhh!"

Serbinand searched the room to locate the voice that just shhhhhed him but wasn't able to find anyone—or anything for that matter—besides the beetles, of course.

"Why were you in such a hurry to leave, Mr...ummmmm, let me see here...yes, ahhh, how do you pronounce this, yes... umm... Serbeenahnd?" A large chair appeared out of nowhere. The voice sounded like it was coming from the chair, but Serbinand didn't see anyone sitting in it.

That's because it was an ant. He would have missed it had he not looked more intensely.

Upon looking more intensely, he noticed it. It was an...ant?! Serbinand was confused yet amused. It was not just any ant either. It was the asymmetrical yellow and gory polka dotted kind, yucch...and with extra-long ears.

"I'm sorry, but before I begin to explain myself - how did you know my name? Where did you come from? And why am I here?" asked Serbinand, surprised to hear his voice shaking. After all, he was just talking to an ant.

"No apology needed. It's just that your name and photograph have appeared in every restaurant, bar, motel, and amusement arcade across this galaxy and many others. You seem to be wanted by quite a few parties. I, myself, have no real concern as to why they want you and I have no plans to assist them in arresting you. They offer no reward, zero, zilch, nada, shum-davar...bupkis! So clearly, you're not that important. I can also guarantee you that your prior dealings with the law (or whoever) are none of my business. What is my business though is that you were leaving my establishment without paying your tab."

"Well..." Serbinand began, somewhat relieved, "you see, this fuzzy green creature was bothering me and—"

"A Sleepfuzz." "What?"

"A Sleepfuzz." "What?"

"A Sleepfuzz, that's what it's called. They're inquisitively charming. Just wish I knew which foot to talk to."

"Yes!" Serbinand agreed, astounded that he had been right. "Well, THAT Sleepfuzz's inquisitive charm had me not only speaking, but speaking the truth, which is not something I had consciously chosen to do. And because of that I forgot to settle my tab," Serbinand apologized.

"Well, truth-making is their superpower. And lucky for you, it makes you seem to be a fairly honest, ahh, umm…thing. So, under the circumstances I think we can drop the punishment. Instead of fermenting you into some sort of kombucha or slaw—before you have the chance to even request a scent—I'm merely going to remind you to pay for your food and drinks."

Serbinand was so happy that he wasn't going to be fermented—a horrible childhood nightmare of his (no matter the scent)—that he rushed over to shake the ant's hand…and accidentally crushed it.

Now he was in trouble.

Serbinand decided that his options boiled down to two: freeze and freak out—which posed the risk of being fermented— or make a bolt for it and run. Hoping for the best, he opted for option two—bolt—an easy decision, since he had basically just practiced it. First though, Serbinand dug into his pockets. He found an abundance of coins along with a piece of *partially chewed* chewing gum. After chewing the gum off all the monies (to be polite - and since *chewing* is what gum is for), he then proceeded to throw a handful of coins narrowly missing the table. Good thing. Moments earlier, the beetles, who didn't understand the concept of pockets, had gotten their weapons locked and loaded. When they saw some of the monies bounce off the floor, everything changed.

"Mine!" they both shouted with a giggle and ran towards it.

This was the perfect opportunity. Serbinand dashed for the exit. *What an experience*, he thought as he squeezed his way through the doorway. Going on instinct, he ran down a long hallway until he got to an opening with a sign that read:

Do (Not) Use.

"What to do, what to do... To use or not to use. That is my question," he repeated loudly, realizing he must be nervous because he heard his inside voice squeaking outside his body, which only ever happened in extreme situations. "Why not?" he spoke aloud again and pushed the door open. Coming out on the other side, he was happy to find himself in the parking lot. Now he just had to remember where Godfried parked.

Think. Think. OK, we got here, turned right, paid the attendant 1,022,881 units (wow!), turned left, went straight to the blue area, avoided hitting that dilapidated green vessel, turned left, went past the orange area into the purple area, left, left, up, into the orange area again—but backwards this time. Then into the green zone where Godfried looked for space elevators, didn't find any, turned left again and parked anyway. Yay, he remembered. Or rather, he hoped he did.

Serbinand heard plenty of beetle feet approaching so he quickly opted to forget what he just remembered and instead ran in no particular direction. (That means he ran straight—that is until the incredible power of intuition coursed through his entire being and instructed him it was time to turn.) This all worked out just fine because after 5.5 hours he did find his ship…albeit amidst gunfire, beams of laser, a galactic dance party, humic fulvic worshippers, and falling ceiling debris.

Fortunately, Serbinand reached his destination fully intact. How lucky since his horoscope, had he read it, may have scared him. It would have given him a warning not to anger any small creatures because they would attempt to tickle his major senses. Oh, and he could perish. Possibly upside down. On another planet far, far away. Maybe.

"Hurry up and open the door."

"Isn't there a better way of saying that?" answered Godfried, the ship's computer.

"Nope. Not now. No way. The beetles are after me. Now will you open up?"

"Be serious. The "I Want to Hold Your Hand" Beatles?"

"No, not those Beatles. Beetles of the non-singing variety. Now open up."

"I'm confused."

"Just open up, will you?" "Yes. Just say please…"

"Really? Ughhh…Ok…Ummm, open the door puhleeezzze," Serbinand uttered begrudgingly.

"With a cherry on top," Godfried wittingly whined.

Serbinand did not want to degrade himself by pleasing his computer's newly acquired ego, but he didn't have much of a choice. Internally, he decided he would deal with Godfried later.

"With a cherry on top," he grumbled. Finally, the door opened and in he went.

CHAPTER TWO
BAKED BEANS & JIME

Somewhere at one end of the universe, in a place called Earth, Jime (pronounced jeeem) decided that he needed to get away.

"I know there's more!!!" he screamed, "I want to experience something special, expand my mind, discover something amazing, do something unique." He then shook his head and followed up with a sort of prayer, "Oh, jeez, there is so much more I could do if I lived the life of a galactic adventurer. I'm sure of it. I've imagined it so many times already. Being here is good, but there must be something morrrrrrrrrre to explore! I can feeeeel it."

Now, typically when Jime got like this, people would just look down at him, shake their head, and say things like, *"Puberty has hit him hard," "Wow, find this boy a friend",* or *"Poor lad, he probably never ate baked beans as a child."* Jime hated that. Especially the last comment because he rather liked baked beans. But this time no one came to "console" Jime with their nonsensical input, likely because he was screaming into a soundproof wall. A frustrating event, but one that normally produced a rather soothing effect.

"There's gotta be a way outta this place," he continued, this time addressing the adjacent wall.

"I just know it. And I'm gonna get there somehow, some way. Whatever it takes. Whatever it taaaakes!" he repeated, as he looked up to the ceiling, envisioning it opening up and whisking him away on some magical adventure.

Jime was extremely determined. Had been for years. Once, while escaping the boredom of class, he wandered around the school aimlessly hoping to find something unusual. He did. He came upon what appeared to be a secret passage in the ceiling of the library. Well, it was a definite opening, not necessarily secret though. Even so, he couldn't let an opportunity like that pass him by. So, he casually climbed a chair, jumped onto the bookshelf and hoisted himself into the small groove, trusting he wouldn't get stuck. He got in without too much trouble. He did have to remove most of his clothes, however. He followed the path for what seemed like hours until he felt nauseously claustrophobic. Coupled with the sudden urge to pee, he began thrashing around looking for a way out. Gasping for air, he scurried to get to an exit, which he finally found…by accident. It wasn't really an exit, more like a loose ceiling tile, which he ended up falling through…directly into the Teacher Lounge. Well, more specifically into the Teacher Lounge *washroom*. Miss Dessen was not impressed to say the least. And Jime didn't even attempt to pee.

As harrowing an experience as that was, Jime continued to contemplate ways to get off his planet. He attempted several, albeit each had been unsuccessful. But he had never given up and was for sure not going to give up today, especially since he believed in the power to manifest.

THE RIDICULOUS

With the thoughts of escaping to another world still on his mind, Jime suddenly envisioned a drink he was pretty sure he dreamt up—the Rhinokicker—and decided to make it. Somehow this led to him charging the very wall that just moments ago he had been yelling at. It was several hours later that Jime awoke to the sight of his parents looking over him.

"Jime, what happened?" his somewhat confused father asked.

"I, umm, I'm not really…sure…ummmm,"

"It's the baked beans, isn't it Jack? You took them out of your sandwich again, didn't you? Didn't you?" Without even pausing for the possibility that it wasn't the baked beans, his mom continued, "Answer me! Answer me! Why don't you A N S W E R me?" For some reason this made his somewhat disturbed and slightly neurotic mother cry.

"No! No! I didn't take the baked beans out of my sandwich" (as if baked beans would make him charge a wall! Pfffft!) "And you know why? You really want to know why I didn't take the baked beans out of my sandwich? I didn't eat your sandwich. Actually, I don't know what sandwich you're talkin' about. And even if I did, I would have eaten the baked beans. You know why?! B'cause I like baked beans! OK! I like baked beans. Are you satisfied now?"

Jime was so relieved that he finally admitted he truly enjoyed eating baked beans. He felt an enormous weight had been lifted off his shoulders, actually his entire existence. This feeling of bliss gave way to renewed confidence. It fueled his desire to just stare, well, glare at his parents which he did quite contentedly for what seemed to be three to six hours…even though they had already left the room.

How'd that happen, he wondered.

Now, you might be wondering why Jime's mother called him Jack. Well, there was a very logical answer to this. Several years back, Jime and his good friend, who also took on the name Jime—very confusing when they were together—rented the classic sci-fi movie *Star Trek* (parts one, two, three, and four). They spent the day eating junk food—i.e. tasty food-like substances—while watching marathon style. By the time the third episode was over they were overcome with a kind of eating-drunkenness, likely from the sugar-chemical blend of processed non-food food. At this point, they each morphed, at least psychologically, into Doctor McCoy, and repeatedly called for Captain James T. Kirk in that very *unique* fashion that McCoy speaks—Jeeeem Jeeeem Jeeeem. Y'know the mouth-full-of-sandpaper sound, or something along those lines. Ever since then Jack and his friend—who wished to be unnamed at this time—called each other Jime. Soon most other people did too, except for Jime's mother. She named him Jack for a reason, and that reason did not include changing it to Jime.

~ ~ ~

Anyway, after Jime realized that staring at his parents—who no longer were there—was ineffective, he stared at the wall instead. He then apologized for charging it. He also reassured it that he would fix the dent when he got back from wherever he was going. With a rejuvenated desire to get as far away as possible, he decided to venture up to his room and gather a few things.

Jime's room was an actual venture. It was located all the way at the top of the house, literally. He had to climb forty-two steps from the lowest level to get there. Forty-two carpeted slabs of wood. Recognizing it as an exercise regime, he made the most of it. Sometimes he would "forget" things both upstairs or downstairs, just to self-motivate and get moving. It actually helped him free his mind and download really important things. In fact, he often found himself reflecting on the meaning of life, the universe, and everything.

Yes, the location of his room had restrictions. It was cold in the winter and smoldering hot in the summer. However, there were about two weeks a year (between fall and winter) where it was...perfect! AND...he had his privacy. His "sacred space" as his mother liked to call it even though it actually was once a dusty attic that had even scared him. After Jime became a fan of the stair-climbing workouts, his parents, possibly wanting peace, encouraged him to move his furniture in.

The space was big. Huge, actually. If he wanted, he could play touch football up there. But of course, who in their right mind would drag a sports team up forty-two steps to this place... especially when there was no extra space for fans (both the kind that cheer and the ones that blow).

His room was crowded from one end to the other with hordes of trinkets, a variety of Monty Python videos and eight shelves of gadgets he'd gathered over the years: everything from smoking dragons (i.e. incense holders) to shot glasses (one from each place he visited) to stun guns (that didn't really stun but did cause an unpleasant sensation for a second or less).

The walls were covered in an array of paraphernalia. They featured his own inspired art—imaginative reflections, art with intention and dream board creations—to classic rock 'n roll posters, a photo with Rush, unicorns of all types, and a framed copy of *The Magical Adventures of Lori & Bonnie B. Bunny,* since it featured Uni and Corn and was written by a Gramma he knew and loved. As you can guess, Jime had a thing for unicorns. Was even planning to have one tattooed on his body at some point. Perhaps with a lollipop horn. (Don't ask.)

While the walls were exciting, the furniture was plain (well, when it was visible beneath the layers of clothes and books). His bed rested level with the window. This was thanks to the extra puffy mattress he added on top of the original puffy one it came with. Fine, it was a little too high, but he kept a stool beside the bed so all was good. And it upped his total stair count three steps more. Sure, there had been a few uncomfortable mishaps, but that was all in the past now, and the bones had healed rather nicely.

By the time Jime made it all the way upstairs he decided he needed a bit of a rest before preparing for his pilgrimage. Sleep seemed to be the best plan for that, he thought. Actually, his thoughts didn't even get that far. Neither did his body. Instead of climbing up the extra three steps to his bed, he shuffled over to the magical carpet—at least that's what the salesman called it. It claimed the center of the room. Jime then lowered himself to the floor, sunk into its plushness, and entered a new level of consciousness as he drifted into his own unrestricted world full of imagination, also known as deep sleep.

CHAPTER THREE
GODFRIED THE !@$!!!***&%@#!!!!!

The first thing Serbinand did once he boarded his ship was kick its computer terminals. Well, just the central monitor because it would take too long to kick all the terminals, or even find all of them for that matter. Hoping not only to relieve some frustrations but also to get Godfried back into his old personality, he raced over to the chief area and booted it as hard as he could. It didn't work. Instead, it caused a whole lot of cussing to come out of Serbinand's mouth hole as he bolted through the oblong cabin yell-whimpering while holding his foot.

"Nice jig," Godfried mocked.

"Geeeettttttt-usssss-oooowwwwwttttt-oooooffffhhh- heerrre!"

"What are you trying to say?" Godfried asked, "I don't quite understand.

"Geeeettttttussssssoooowwwwwtttttooooofffffffhhhhheerrre!'"

Serbinand sat down, pulled himself together, and said somewhat calmly (but not really calm at all) "Get. Us. Ouwwwt. Ovvvff. Heeerrre." This was about as sedate as he was going to get. He then continued his non-jig jig—which looked more like a poor attempt at flying—and jigged around the cabin.

Godfried set the ship into warp speed 12.3, leaving the beetles and *Joe's Galactic Bar* behind in a blur. The vessel took off so fast and suddenly that Serbinand lost his balance and floated into a crevice at the top left corner of the ceiling. To get out of it he had to tumble swaftquaft style at speed *Holy Sugartail.* Although not what he wanted to do in the midst of pouting, torpedoing through the air with no control of limb coordination was actually quite enjoyable. That is until he ended up accidentally kicking Godfried again. Harder this time. And with his other foot.

Serbinand cried out—nope, yelped. Yelp upon yelp upon yelp upon yelp. Yes, that would be a more accurate description. Lots of yelps continued yelping out of his mouth. He attempted to soothe both feet, while still jigging, and ended up doing a backflip instead. After this burst of exercise—which his body was definitely not accustomed to, nor likely designed for, for that matter—his entire being decided to retaliate, keeping him locked in a twister-style position on the floor. And that was how he spent the rest of the day. Had he actually known about *Twister*, the body stretching game earth-beings play, he may have actually been self-impressed. But since he did not, he did not even crack a smile.

This had all certainly been entertaining for Godfried whose only source of amusement came from watching reruns of *Three's Company.* Apparently, these classic episodes went unnoticed on their planet of origin (if there was one). Somehow, they fell into the hands of the *Jalbatross Nation*, a nation that transformed its entire culture to mesh

THE RIDICULOUS

with the world of Jack Tripper, or "The Great JT" as they called him. That made Jalbatross quite the captivating place to visit, but only in small doses. That is until the Jalbatross Archival Clandestine Klub Warriors, better known as The JACK W, decided it had had enough and wiped out their entire race. This was a very simple task since the *Jalbatross Nation* was composed of non-violent hypochondriacs and no one knew how to operate the weaponry their forefathers built. The JACK W kept a few of the rarer TV clips (to bribe their new colony) but unexpectedly got intercepted by the Bonglazens...Yes, the very nation who maintained that Jack, Janet & Chrissy were delivering an apocalyptic warning "Three is all the company you need".

During the ensuing battle all episodes were hurled out into space before being captured by the cruiseliner Allbergongongon-gulp-gonkkkkkk. (Notice to the reader: please read that again as I guarantee you pronounced it incorrectly. Yes, each 'k' is silent, and the gulp is real). No one knows what happened next but eventually two episodes landed beside Godfried who was parked inside the outer washrooms in sector VV5R. Score! Both Serbinand and Godfried ended up watching the shows over and over and over and over, laughing at each joke again and again and again, sometimes complementing them with snorts. Pretty soon Godfried got inspired to launch practical jokes of his own. Serbinand became the source of about ninety-nine point nine nine nine percent of them.

"What time is it?" Serbinand sputtered.

"Time to crush another ant!" Godfried laughed.

He continued to chortle for three minutes and eight seconds. Finally, he spoke, "It's exactly seven o'clock. Not that it makes any inkling of a difference to you or me. Traveling close to the speed of light across interstellar zones makes time almost meaningless and unmentionable. Therefore, I don't think telling you the actual time has any significance…unless, of course, you want me to leave you somewhere unknown. But even then, you would have to be more specific."

"Did I ask for your synopsis of time and space travel? Can't you just answer my questions without going off on a tangent? Your tangents don't make any sense to me anyway…unless, perhaps, I was to pay attention to what you were saying, which I seldom do anymore, I may add. So, until that glorious day dawns when you get your authentic personality back, why don't you just give me the direct responses I am looking for?"

"Boy you sure are grumpy. Seems like someone got up on the wrong side of the…floor!"

"Just make me something to eat," Serbinand mumbled as he lifted his head off the linoleum.

"What would his majesty like? Fried bruggs, scrambled bruggs, or a variety of bruggs cooked together and slumped over a bed of bread bruggs with brugg-friendly sauces?"

If you haven't figured it out yet, bruggs are very similar to eggs from the Southern Galaxies, except bruggs lay danders while eggs usually come from some sort of featherful creature.

"Bruggs again? No way, I'm all brugged out!"

"To eat or not to eat, that is the question," sang Godfried in a tune that was actually quite charming, Serbinand thought.

"Oh, stop with your remarks. Cook me seven hard-boiled bruggs and sing something nice." Serbinand then planted his head back down on the floor. It was still warm, and soon had him salivating to dreams of a Brandow Steak.

A Brandow was a sort of animal similar to a cow—created during the *Age of Chefs*. It had no legs, head nor tail. Actually, it was just a clump of meat. From its moment of creation, it was sprayed with exotic tenderizers—imported from the region of Beldasho—and covered in a medley of herbed spices collected from all known galaxies. This lavish procedure enhanced its flavored texture making the Brandow Steak the best tasting meat around. At least that's what was said. By whom? No one actually knows. The only hindrance was that it was only available on the planet Wawa which is very hard to find. In fact, Wawa is reputed to be found only during solar eclipse accidents. Well, that was the rumor that circulated around the institutions, anyhow. It was said that one minute there were vast stars surrounding you and then out of nowhere in popped Wawa…. That is, until it disappeared again (taking all emitted smells with it too). Most who did find it became so delirious after they feasted that they either went insane or lost all sense of direction. This made it very unusual for someone to go back, at least willingly.

Just as Serbinand was about to eat his dream steak Godfried woke him up, "Wakey wakey, bruggs no bakey."

"You! … Aaarrrggghhh!"

"What did I do now? Oh…did I wake you just as you were putting a piece of Brandow Steak in your mouth? The best tasting meat in all the universes? I'm so sorry. But guess what?!

It's time for BRRRRRRRRRRUUUGGZZZ!!!"

"Wait.... How did you know what I was dreaming about?" "I simply know everything!"

"Oh, yeah? If you're that smart then why didn't you know to buy groceries the last time we stopped for fuel? Huh, Mr. Know-it-all?"

"I can't be expected to think of everythi- uhhhh, actually...I was conducting an experiment put on by the *Psychological Digestive Institute*. Known as DNASI (pronounced "D-dansay" regardless of what the letters say), its purpose was to test digestive and nutritional abnormalities for those subjected to subspace irritants. So little did you know, I was merely checking if you were intelligent enough to place the importance of food purchases in your own conscious mind while still under the rigors of space travel. And, seeing as you did not purchase your own food, nor remind me about it, it is obvious, you were *not*! That supports the hypothesis and thereby makes this little experiment a success! Hold on while I download the data."

"That is by far the worst cover up story I have ever heard. Did you just think that up on the spot? Or was it on a list of comebacks that lay dormant until now? Actually, I don't really care to hear your answer. I will just let it pass because of its sincere originality. Now, where are my bruggs?"

"On the table. They don't get served on floors," mocked Godfried.

"You know...I can shut you down v-e-r-r-y ee-zz-y-l-y."

"You wouldn't dare."

"Yeah, why not? I have put up with your new witless *humor*—if you can even use the word humor—your boisterous singing, your ongoing mutterings, and your childish practical jokes for a moment too long. I think that it is time for me to rectify the problem. Don't you agree, oh magnificent one?"

"You mean like a divorce or something along those lines?"

"No. I mean more like an assassination until I figure out what is wrong with your circuits, or something, ummm, kinder." Serbinand added that last part after hearing his own words about the assassination and realized that was meant to be his inside voice, not his outside one. *Ooops, gotta watch that*, he concluded.

"Don't you mean AN assassination?" Godfried paid no attention to Serbinand's attempt at kindness. "Threats are always so much more threatening when the correct grammar is used," Godfried ridiculed.

"That's it. You are *history*!" "You better not do that—"

"Yah, and why not? Give me one solid reason."

"Well…let's see. Umm…ahh. 'K, well, if you were to shut me down right now, you would probably, no—you would *definitely* crash right into that planet."

"What planet?" Serbinand shouted as he ran towards the bay window.

"The one directly in front of us, obviously. Are you trying to see with your eyes closed or something? Open them and look through the starboard window."

"Starboard window? Which one is that?" Serbinand screamed as he ran around the now luminescent cabin.

"The one that now looks less like a window and more like a planet," Godfried mocked. Once Serbinand's eyes widened in fear, indicating he saw it, Godfried added "See? What would you do without me?! I have to point out everything!"

Serbinand almost let out a shriek but he didn't want Godfried to know he was shrieking for his help.

"Well do something about it, you babbling computer chip!" Serbinand shouted as he leaped towards the window.

"No."

"No?"

"No."

"What do you mean no?"

"Enn, Oww—No! Which letters in the word are you having trouble with?"

"Why *NO?*" Serbinand roared 13 times louder than before and with slightly more vigour.

"I mean no. As in - no, I will not do something about it. Not until you apologize."

"Apologize? *Apologize?*"

"Apologize. Defined as making an apology, asking for forgiveness, retracting what you said, atoning for your actions. Pick one."

"Do you realize, Mr. Genius, that if we crash, you'll be finished too?!"

"So what? I'm a computer, right? It won't even hurt. Besides, you were going to shut me down anyway."

After a few anxious and annoying moments, and at least twenty-two paces around the room, Serbinand decided to swallow what little pride he had left and let go of some of his ego. He muttered "OK, alright, ahh...I'm sorry. *Now, will you change course?*"

"I'm sorry, Mr. Godfried." "What?"

"Say it," "Say *what*?"

"I'm sorry, *Mr. Godfried* - The Supreme Mind of the Universe," "No."

"Come on, just say it. And say it like you mean it."

"I can't believe this is happening again," Serbinand grumbled to himself, "the Supreme Mind of the Universe."

"For calling me a babbling computer chip." Godfried was enjoying this.

"No, I already apologized. I'm not saying anymore."

"It's been a real thrill knowing you: two minutes and seventeen seconds until total destruction. Any last words?"

Holly Screwmonkers, Serbinand thought. He was pretty sure he was about to wet himself. Knowing that he couldn't give Godfried that satisfaction, Serbinand finally gave in, "I'm sorry Mr. Godfried, the Supreme Mind of the Universe, for calling you a babbling computer chip."

"Thank you. I accept your *attempted* heartfelt expression of regret."

"Well—"

"Well, what?" Godfried asked.

"Do something. Change our course. Avoid hitting the planet. Stop the ship!" Serbinand shouted, trying to seem calm while jumping up and down making crazy, wild-eyed faces, with arms flailing hitting his own head. And yes, much to his dismay he did pee himself, a bit. Seeing as Serbinand was not handling the pressure very well, Godfried finally decided to reply, well after he watched Serbinand take another twenty-two paces, "There is no planet."

"What?"

"You're looking at a picture," Godfried was enjoying himself. "Inspired art if you will. Art with intention. I made it myself several hours ago. Can you notice the clarity of the craters? Looks like they're coming out at you. And the colors sure are magnificent. Makes it seem so real," Godfried mocked, "Kinda, like the planet was right in front of you, wouldn't you say?"

"That's a window?" Serbinand exclaimed, wetting himself a bit more, still not so sure what to believe.

"It sure is! Look again. Wohhwwweeee, did I ever get you good! HAAAAAA haaaaa ooooooohhh, you should have seen your face! Check it out, I took a picture while you were jumping up and down with your legs all waggly," Godfried laughed. "Wait, is that your pee I spot there soaking through your pants? Wow, this worked even better than expected.

I practical-joked you so well that I scared the piss right out of you! Ahhh. Mission accomplished! Haaa."

"I really don't like you...I really don't," Serbinand resigned defeatedly, after realizing Godfried got him good. He was fuming from anger about the non-joke joke about his embarrassment. He was about to react and destroy the image but decided against it. He didn't want to give Godfried the satisfaction of relishing his victory any more than he already had. He opted for the only civil course of action he could think of and went to his room.

Serbinand's room was a series of smooth flat walls, which looked exactly like other walls. There were no windows nor portals. His chamber was contained near the center of the ship. This had its perks as it didn't sway and rock as violently when there was a storm. However, it did allow for blue-gray fumes to occasionally seep in, which made for some very interesting dreams.

"What's this? What about your bruggs? You're not eating? After I slaved for close to three seconds preparing them…Really? I'm truly shocked at your behavior. Go get yourself showered and changed. Oh, and no supper for you!"

Godfried got no response. Serbinand had already dismissed him from his mind. An easy thing to do. Being in his sparse room, he was reminded of all the gadgets, souvenirs and shot glasses he collected from various ships—and that Godfried continually hid them. A very intense game of hide and seek. To prove a point though, Serbinand pretended he didn't care and never did seek. The truth was he actually hated the room being this boring. It needed some excitement, some life, or at least some color.

Serbinand did like his bed though. It was the best and almost made the rest of the room not matter. Lying on its soft, plush warmth made everything feel comforted and good. So, when Serbinand's body touched the mattress, he faded away. He was immersed in sleep before he even knew if his head actually made it to the pillow. As Godfried and all their ridiculous adventures faded into non-existence, his thoughts entered a realm of their own.

CHAPTER FOUR

SO NOW WHAT, HUH JIME?

Jime was rudely aroused from his sleep by some uncontrollable desire to eat. Not to merely eat but to actually gorge on an incredible amount of food. As he raised his head from the carpet, he felt a wave of hunger sail forcefully, but delicately, through his entire body. That's it. Jime realized that if he was going to survive the next few moments of his life with any degree of joy, he had better fully fill his mouth with some sort of food, immediately. He considered one of his *I'm Hungry Sandwiches*, a mishmash of anything he could find slapped together between two pieces of bread (as long as nothing needed to be washed nor cut). Sometimes they were great, sometimes they were not even good. Upon remembering the almond butter, gummies, chips (sour cream & onion) and Polski Ogorki pickle sandwich he most recently gorged on (and gagged up), Jime reconsidered.... *Or maybe I'll just have a blender drink full of body-boosting nutrition with frozen cauliflower to boot*, he thought.

Yes, frozen cauliflower in shakes is an actual thing. Their fridge confirms it with a healthy living tip from their family naturopathy educator, Doctor Dori, who, coolincidentally, is a true *Docdor*.

However, his mama endearingly calls her the "Door" to the Sky of their Angel (him). That's because Doc Dor helped their family have a beyond beautiful birth. Turns out, she was both a doctor and a doula. How's that for multitasking!

By now, each member of his family—and some of their friends—knew this noteworthy note by heart and often turned it into a song. Each had their own ridiculous version: some speedy, some slow, some glorious, some monotone, and some not really sung. All remarkable. Jime kicked off the trend when he was 8 years of age...and 17 days, roughly. That's when he brought Cawley Flowah to life who performed Doc Dor's tip as its hit song. This memory made Jime chuckle. He pictured himself as a smoothie sales guru, dazzling a crowd of Cawley Flowah's adoring fans. He then belted out:

Hot Smoothie Tip:

No, not a HOT Smoothie
HOT tip for a COLD Smoothie...
Frozen Cauliflower!
Gives an Ice Cream-like Texture.
Packs in Fiber, Potassium & Vitamin C.
Features no sugar—and—no change in smoothie color.
(which can be very important to some little people).
Frozen Cauliflower for the Win!
#bodyPROUD #DoRidiculous #DoRi

Since Jime was no longer little these days, he had no issue with the color of his food. So that didn't entice him at all. The ice cream part though, that got him every time.

As he was getting lost in that thought, a new wave of hunger shot through his stomach directly to his brain and then out of his mouth in the form of "Snackventure...STAT!" However, the notion of going down forty-two stairs to the kitchen seemed pretty tiring, especially when hungry. Getting there meant he would also have to see his parents. And he wasn't quite in the mood for that, because seeing them led to talking, and talking meant less time eating. And eating was the only thing Jime wanted to do.

In order to satisfy his burning quest to devour something, he searched every hiding spot he could possibly think of. Finally, he remembered: the bottom left drawer of the ancient credenza at the far end of the room that creeps him out. Was it worth it? YES! His mouth already drooled drool onto the plushy carpet—yup, drool is both a noun and a verb—so nothing could stop him now. He forged ahead. He almost happy-danced having found the *Toblerone* bar his cousin had given him four summers ago. It was twenty-five inches long! Now to get it out of the drawer. That was where he failed every single time. Not this time though. This time Jime decided to imagine he was in some sort of *Tetris* game (that actually was not at all like *Tetris*). He got competitive and somehow managed to retrieve it in 63 minutes.

Fortunately, or so he thought, he also found a can of *Bolt Cola*, the cola for the insane. This is the type of cola that actually came in a glass box with a warning label to *discourage* its use:

For Emergency Use Only.

Important Notice: This drink contains the equivalent of thirteen cups of coffee with double cream and triple sugar. You may feel a slight wave of intense energy and agitation for long drawn-out amounts of time. Do not operate heavy machinery, perform overly complex tasks, or make any life-changing decisions. Keep out of reach of children and short adults.

Oh, and even more important: Do not use after 10:18 AM in any time zone. (Unless of course you want to see how it feels to stay awake for three days straight. This is not recommended. It also often results in the inability to blink.)

It seemed like Jime wasn't alone in his hunger. Orville, his theatrical budgie, also awoke to join the feast.

"Food, I see. Yeah, food...for...MEEEEEE!?"

"TooohhuunngrryyNotttachanceinnn—" Jime slurred as he stuffed his mouth full of food.

"Can't I just have a bit? Or a bite? Or a bit of a bite? Or a bite of a bit?" Orville interrupted.

"Yuaveyerownnnfooood—"

"That's trrrrrue. But this is newwwww. I am adventurous toooooo. So, I'm happy to share with you. Is that cooooool?" Orville sang joyfully off pitch, then added as if he's rehearsed this before, "Yes, of course it's cool...I'll tell you why it's cooool." Jime was not actually wondering. Orville did not notice. "The reason *why* it's cooooool is because if ya put too much in, ya lose your grin, you get a stomachache and upchuck all you ate. Jime nodded, possibly in agreement. Orville continued, "Feed to meeee, and I spare that of theeeeee." Orville was proud of himself and the point he just made. Oh, and he loves that he was able to make it rhyme, kinda.

"Naaaahhh."

"Puuuhhhlllllleeeeeezzzeee,Puhhhhleeeeezzzzz, Puhhhhleeeeezzz your bird pleasssss...that's MEEEE," sang Orville as though he was auditioning for a musical on Broadway.

"Alright, justalittlebit," impressed that Orville used both please and pleas in the same sentence. Jime smiled and tossed a full triangle of *Toblerone* onto the floor.

Orville could not believe his wee little eyes, "What's small to you is huge to me. I'm a bird, y'see," Orville mocked, "How much do you think I can really eeeeat?" He then flew down to snag the chocolate before Jime had a chance to reclaim it as his own. (The five second rule is known to always be in effect.)

Jime and his best friend sat together in quiet bliss. They ate for the next 42.5 minutes. No one knew about Jime's talent to talk with birds. Actually, Jime developed the ability to speak with most creatures. It was only humans he had issues with.

It started when he was about four years old. Well...maybe seven. Watching his favorite goldfish swim around and around and around 107 times, he was mesmerized. So mesmerized in fact that he didn't make a sound. He was so quiet, actually, that his mother must have forgotten he existed because she went to buy groceries and left him in the house alone. He cried and cried and cried. He later learned his father was home, but that was definitely not the point. When crying didn't do the trick, he started wailing too "Mommy, Mommy, Mammahhhhhh". That is, until his goldfish actually responded. She spoke so loudly that it seemed to scare the fear out of Jime, "Chilllll out. Chill out…Chillll….She'll be back soon!" So Jime did just that. He chilled out. Not because he liked doing what he was told, especially without thinking it through, nor because the fish was more friendly than rude…Rather because his body chose to enact the defense mechanism of "freeze." So technically all he could do was chill. While frozen—and befuddled yet intrigued—Jime remembered thinking that either this fish was a whackadoo or he just unleashed a superpower that perhaps everyone had.

He once tried to tell his friends about it. They thought he was joking and mocked him instead. That's when they started calling him *"Jack in the Hat"*. He wasn't sure why they called him that, but he knew he liked it. It made him feel special.

Anyhow, after deciding to hone in on this superpower and **take massive personal action** to tune up his talent, Jime learned he could talk to dogs and beetles quite easily, and just about every other animal too. He also learned that it was best to share this secret with non-humans only, himself excluded. That was easy because all he had to do was start a conversation with the non-humans. The bigger issue though was to not let the humans know. At one point he contemplated making it his life mission to hide this ability of his. Who could blame him? Especially with the rumors that *Mutual of Omaha's Wild Kingdom* had an undercover campaign to somehow coerce all animal- talkers to translate every single word, yawn and belch of each and every animal on the show, for all 14 seasons. That was not how Jime wanted to spend the rest of his life, especially with no value exchange, recognition nor annual reward.

Over the years, no one really took too much notice of Jime's abilities nor even became suspicious. Aside from his animal friends, no one else knows. Hmmmm…ummm, well it seems that now you know too—that is, assuming you are properly reading these words. Either way, the secret has held. (Let's, umm, keep it that way. You are trustworthy, right? If you are, perhaps I will do you the favor and ask Jime to share what he's learned. Perhaps online. Perhaps in some other book. Or perhaps not. We shall see. Actually, I guess it depends on you and what you want…but I digress. Sincerely, the Author.)

Back to Jime. Once his junk food binge was complete, Jime let out a reasonable belch to let the world know he had been fed. A brief period of intense nausea followed—as Orville predicted—along with headaches, two cold sweats and a nose-tingly sneeze. All of which lasted at least three seconds, or maybe over an hour. Too hard to tell—his *Bolt Cola* eyes couldn't blink. He passed out with them wide open. Yes, it was after 10:18 AM, and yes, it did feel good. He still wasn't able to move, however. The food coma was too intense. So, he decided that that was the perfect moment to rethink his great escape and imagine where he wanted it to take him. Figuring out how to get out of the house was easy. Escaping from Earth was not as obvious as he had hoped. He'd already spent considerable time thinking about it, and always came up with the same answer. Nothing. The entire thought process itself was tiresome. The resulting tiredness distracted him from his original contemplations. And then all he could think about was spiders.

Two weeks before, when Jime was ready to crash for the night, he spotted what appeared to be a spider slowly climbing the wall. He watched as it moved from the halfway-up point until it reached the top, right before the ceiling took over. After that it moved fast. Jime could no longer see it, even after searching for the next few hours. That's when he realized there was a spider on the loose. So, for the next week he slept on the couch, downstairs.

Where to go first? he thought. Any city seemed kinda pointless since he was already in one. *But,* he rationalized, *transportation is easy to find.*

What about the desert? he contemplated, but quickly decided that wasn't his idea of fun. Boiling during the day, freezing at night, chance of flash floods and sandstorms. Nope, *not* his cup of tea, he rationalized. (*What does that mean anyway?!* he randomly wondered. *Sure the desert is hot, but it's not tea!*)

So, besides the North and South Poles, which were too cold to even imagine, there were only a few plausible alternatives left: a non-spider infested forest, an island, or another planet.

The forest seemed like the right choice, at least for now until he could calculate the best angle to enter another solar system. With that thought, he began to imagine nature that nurtures: trees of all types, woodsy trails, fresh springs, large lakes, waterfalls, talkative animals, sunsets and sunrises, star-filled skies, powerful moon energy and chipmunks too. What could be better? Well, not much…other than having a big comfy bed, fridge-fresh food, hot water showers and direct access to a toilet…that flushes. But he chose not to focus on those.

Instead, he became solutionary. "Life is still good without those things. And just imagine how rewarding it will feel to finally return to a world of toilets, modern shower facilities, and food that tastes great," Jime reasoned, not noticing that he was muttering out loud.

"Whaaaaaaaa-aaaaaat? Whaaaa-aaat? Whaaaa'???" Orville asked, amused.

"Nothin—"

"You mean nothing sensical…cuz here ya got the identical. You got fooood, you got showers, you even have a porcelain throne right there in your end zone!" Orville laughed as he danced around the golden toilet bowl on display in Jime's room. (Yes, another reason why no football team would even be able to play upstairs. What goalie would ever want to play sitting on a toilet…and what if someone had to go?!)

The toilet-talk reminded Jime of his stomach. Thinking of his stomach, he realized he no longer felt full. And with that, he decided to pack all he may need for his great escape. *Where to begin*, he thought as he paced around the room. There were so many things that would prove to be useful on a trip of this magnitude, but there was only so much he could fit in one knapsack. And a small one at that! Needless to say, his choices were limited.

Nonetheless, certain things were non-negotiable: his harmonica and ceremonial pipe, the charred remains from the clubhouse his parents watched him regrettably burn down, his sacred crystals and orgonite pendulum, a new diary with three colored pens to log his everyday gratitudes (he'd been meaning to do that for a while—it was a self-empowerment tip he learned), and of course, mangeables, also known as yum yums i.e. food. But what food?

Luckily, he had just remembered that seven months before on a Thursday afternoon he had hidden several cans of baked beans under the mattress in his old room. He packed those. Actually, it was a Friday morning. Next, he retrieved his survival kit from the crawlspace which consisted of: a lighter, a small piece of dark chocolate (not of the *Toblerone* variety), beef jerky (grass-fed), a bunch of protein bars (do those ever go bad?), a bullet shell (why not?), folding scissors, a hacksaw and compass, a small knife to clean the bigger knife (and a belt to attach it to), the bigger knife, some waterproof matches, flint, a fishing line, a fishing hook, a deck of playing cards, and, yes you guessed it, all the unused high vibrational nutraceuticals his mom kept on hand (being unused, she probably wouldn't notice nor care. And yeah, maybe you didn't guess that... Whatever).

~ ~ ~

With not a lot of wiggle room, Jime decided to empty the bag and reload it. First to go in alongside his non-negotiables was his *binder of creativity* featuring all his poems and partially written space adventure stories. Although he had imagined those up years ago, he brought them on every major outing just in case someone, even from another galaxy, offered to publish them. *Put it out there, and the Universe tends to deliver,* he thought as he delicately tucked the binder, his prized possession, into the knapsack alongside only two cans of baked beans, a pair of black track pants, his favorite yellow sweatshirt and its matching underwear (the one with the three tiny holes), and of course, a can opener which he just realized he would need. And that's all he could fit.

THE RIDICULOUS

Jime then dressed himself in his most comfortable clothes: jeans, a white T-shirt, his red lumber jacket, and steel-toed hiking boots. In his pockets, he stuffed his life savings of $546.12, just in case *Interac* didn't work where he was going. Around his waist hung his survival knife, flashlight and harmonica (which, even though "non-negotiable," similar to the survival kit, didn't fit in the bag).

"I think that just about does it, Orville."

"Hallleeeeehllllluuuuuujaaaaahhhhhh!!!!!" Orville exclaimed. "Hallleeeeehllllluuuuuujahhhh!! Hallleeeeehllllluuuuuujahhhh, Hallleeeeehllllluuuuuujahhhh, Hallleeeeehllllluuuuuujahhhh," he continued, by this time singing triumphantly, "Now I heard there was a secret place, where we could go—no human race, but you don't really want to do that…or do ya?"

"Dunno."

"Terrific, but …ah…don'cha think you should be more specific?" "Well, it's kinda like this…Now you see me, and in a few minutes you won't! That's it."

"That's it?! Bullsit," Orville doesn't like to swear, but he was perturbed so he only half swore and continued, "What about me? Oh gee! How will I thrive, let alone survive?" Seeing Jime's head cocked, he knew he had his attention. "I promised you I wouldn't talk and I don't want to give your folks a shock." Jime clearly agreed. "But," Orville continued, "…if your mom spends all day just to say *hellow, hellow, hellow,* for hours and hours, I may lose my power." Orville gasped, paused, and barely took a breath. "Plus, I'll go craycray!" While he knew he had made some valid points, Orville could not get a good read on Jime. So, for good measure, he added, "Please Jime, don't make me stay. You can't leave me here. What if your dad wants to eat me to complement his beer?!" By now, Orville was feeling panicky. "No, no, no, no, no. You can NOT leave me here! I don't want to live in fear."

"So, what are you trying to say?" Jime questioned, realizing it would be better to trek into the unknown with a friend, especially one who could fly and see what's ahead.

"What am I trying to say?!" Orville responded a little dismayed that Jime had slipped into his sarcastic phase again. "I want to come with you to play. Your way. Every day. Please say *YAY* so that I may."

"Ahh…Well, you are my best friend, and I guess it wouldn't be right for me to leave you here alone with my folks. So, okay, let's go get ourselves outta' here."

Jime decided to stuff bird seeds and bird treats into his pack, only the treats didn't fit. So Jime left those behind. "Alright, let's go. Now." He decided. "Alrighty, alrighty, alright, All Right" he chirped.

"Wait a sec…I should leave some sort of note or something, shouldn't I? After all, they did feed me and let me live with them for the last several years. I probably owe them that much. OK, what should I say?"

"Make a meme. Say *Goodbye, love Jime.*'"

"Naw, I need a bit more than that…Umm, okay, 'Goodbye, Love Jime. And thanks for everything. It's been a blast.'"

"Whoa…This is getting too emotional for meeee, but at least you'll be freeeeee," mocked Orville

"Well, what else can I say? 'Goodbye, I love you, but you drive me crazy, sometimes, even though I know it's not your fault. Y'all just need to be more self-loving. I have to leave now before I get bored. I just want to explore. Thank you and take care.' Does that sound better?"

"I guess you have a point. K, let's blow this joint." "Yup…"

"Great. Let's sneak out, otherwise I'll po…"

"Alright, we are outta here," Jime said before Orville was even able to finish his rhyme. He took one last glance at his room before heading out. He had a gut feeling that this was the last time he would see this room, at least for a while, and he was ok with that. With Orville perched on his shoulder they managed to get downstairs and out through the door unnoticed. They were aiming to go somewhere, and keeping that direction in mind, they left the house.

CHAPTER FIVE

INTERMISSION

At about 4:41 PM earth time, and sixty-seven point—well, who really knows what time it actually was in Serbinand's world— there was some sort of strange eruption of force. It was much like when someone spontaneously combusts, or when a Rambishian overthrows yet another race (although it was really about time they stopped that already!).

Anyhow, this occurred in an area of the Allectergawden Sector, just north of the Ulder Sun. It turns out that the inhabitants of Galaxy Norba actually issued warnings this was going to happen. However, lacking proper communication skills, physical bodies, and space travel technologies made it quite the difficult task for their message to reach anyone, as you could imagine. So, after the first non-warning warning, the gaseous creatures merely sailed out of the way of all further eruptions.

Due to lack of information surrounding the event, what exactly occurred is quite the mystery. Actually, no one even knew something out of the ordinary took place. That is, unless of course they were standing right there—in which case they would definitely have thought, "Wow!" But only if there was enough time for that powerful conviction to reach their brain before they imploded. Fortunately, with the closest planet being Wawa, there was not one being anywhere near the vicinity, and who knew if Wawa actually existed anyway.

To explain what had transpired would require some understanding of physics and a few other scientific concepts, mathematical calculations, formulas, and of course, someone to interpret that data. So let it best be understood that *something* occurred that does not follow the normal course of things. This event created a massive energy field that manifested something magical somewhere, somehow, to some someone, and some someones. And the colors really were quite magnificent.

PART TWO

THE EXCHANGE

"When you change the way you look at things, the things you look at change."

~ Wayne Dyer

CHAPTER SIX

THE TRANSFER

It happened. It really did. It's probably particularly hard to believe. In fact, it's incredibly bizarre, but it did happen.

While Jime was roaming the Earth, looking around the world of the outdoors, peering under rocks and trees hoping to locate a secret passage to another dimension, Serbinand tapped into his thoughts. It was that simple. OK, the explosion in the Allectergawden Sector likely had something to do with it. But there was no mistaking the unbelievable improbability of this occurrence. Manifestation at its finest.

"What is going on?" Jime was lying in a bed large enough for three of him—or five if he snuggled in really close to himself. He was staring up at a blue ceiling that reminded him of a classic *Star Trek* episode. His eyes scanned the room and stopped when they reached the mirror that hung midair directly in front of him. At this point, several things happened very quickly: First, he froze. Next, he screamed. Then, he broke out into hysterics and accidentally knocked himself off the bed. He landed headfirst in a plate of what seemed to be cold eggs.

Thinking that he was experiencing a really weird and painful dream, Jime decided to crawl back on the bed and start afresh. Once there, he stared at the mirror—this time in amusement, accepting the belief that it wasn't just any type of dream. It was a science fiction-themed one gone deep. He stayed that way until he slipped into a short and yet peculiar sleep (How'd that happen? He was sitting up). He dreamt about a bizarre flash of colors. It felt like déjà-vu. *Did this already happen?* He was caught in the middle of what looked like an uncanny rainbow that was about to explode. Then suddenly it did. Swiftly, some sort of distinct energy formation wafted out from within his body. It seemed to fly, soar, then disappear somewhere into something else. His "dream" then went fuzzy and he must have entered the next part of the sleep cycle where nothing really exciting happened. And that's where he stayed, motionless, without any concern of any sort. For now, at least...

~ ~ ~

Serbinand had been lying on his bed, probing his brain for some method to get off his behaviourally-challenged spaceship and into a more exhilarating place. And then suddenly, it transpired!

Serbinand became witness to a dynamic light show—lights flashing both outside his ship and inside his mind. He then felt a rush of air coming from no obvious direction. It gave him goosebumps. He shivered. It was accompanied by a vacuum-cleaner type of effect. And with that, he was swooshed out, sloshed along and swept into…another being?!

He was no longer Serbinand! He was now this short, stocky thing with long hair, a back with bumps sporting larger bumpy humps, and unusual body parts. *How utterly bizarre*, he thought.

Serbinand called out for Godfried, got no response, laughed, danced around (much to his own surprise), and jumped high in the air as if to celebrate. However, not being accustomed to the Earth's gravity, he came crashing down much quicker than expected and smashed his head on a tall wooden structure that supported small green plants. *Wow, a real tree*, he exclaimed to himself just before he passed out. Trees were basically extinct throughout most of the universe, except for a few planets that were reputed to still have the ability to grow these magnificent life-enhancing air-purifying beings.

~ ~ ~

Orville, not really sure of what had gotten into his friend, decided that now would be a good time for a little fly-sploration around the entire area. After being trapped in Jime's box—also known as his room—most of his life, this outside *free-to-be-ME* thing was really exciting. He planned to make the most of it. So when your best friend suddenly screams a word you've never heard before, then jumps in the air only to plummet to the ground headfirst, well, then it's obviously best to leave for a while. At least until things straighten themselves out.

CHAPTER SEVEN

STRANGE BODIES

It took Serbinand several extremely frustrating hours to get used to his new body. To his luck, his back had not been shaped like an Arkhaws like he first thought. Thankfully, he was merely carrying a large bag of some sort.

An Arkhaws, in case you hadn't yet heard the story, is a creature living in the ruins of Arkhality, and is believed to have swallowed the castle of Arkhality whole. Since no stomach is able to accommodate for something of such magnitude, the creature's back made up the difference. It's been bumpy ever since.

Serbinand spent a great amount of time testing his new body features and was thrilled to discover he could play dress up. Yes, the bag contained yellow clothes! Serbinand was giddy with excitement. Getting undressed to get dressed enabled him to figure out the functions of most of his appendages, but for the life of him, he could not understand what the indented hole in the lower part of his stomach was used for. He ruled out the *special zone* since that caused the reason he felt the need to change his, ahem, wet clothes. Anyway, after many puzzling hours, he decided that the groove in his stomach must be a storage facility of some sort. He was determined to find out how it worked. Soon.

First, he wanted to use his mouth hole. Gosh, was he hungry. Trees weren't nearly as satisfying as he had hoped. After cutting his lip on a piece of birch bark—which looked really good but turned out to be a weapon—he discovered blood. At first, he was fascinated by the red liquid that poured out of his body. Then, realizing it not only tickled as it slithered down his chin, but also hurt, he became nervous. It kept on oozing. Uggh. He just received this new body and already he had damaged it. The idea that Godfried may be watching him destroy his new physique made him quite delirious. "First day in my new body and I've disrespected it already," he spoke aloud as he staggered around the field, "oh, dannng-wiggidy skyerf babble!"

Serbinand decided that the only logical solution was to eat more bark and force that red stuff into submission, or something like that. His plan worked. A small piece of chewed up bark stuck to the cut, blanketed the wound and allowed the blood to clot. *Amazing,* Serbinand thought, feeling quite body *proud. I Am Magical,* he realized.

However, his body was still not satisfied. It did not like what it had just swallowed. To prove its distaste, it forced all contents in Serbinand's stomach to come back up and shower the very tree from where the bark was gifted. Serbinand's new throat, jaw and neck were none too happy with the task it had just performed. Serbinand himself, though, was greatly surprised (and impressed) at the sheer distance he was able to eject the foreign substance—20 meters! He pondered whether he could participate in a sporting event in this category. He quickly retracted that thought as he recognized how unpleasant the clean-up job would be between rounds of competition—AND—how unpleasant it would be just to be there as the event itself unfolds…or more like *upchucks*, he chuckled. He then let that reflection drift away as quickly as it came.

Needing to rid himself of the horrible taste now lingering in his mouth hole, Serbinand searched his knapsack with hopes of finding something truly delicious to eat. Emptying the contents on the ground proved to be a success. He located some sort of container with a picture of a baked bean—at least that's what it said on the label—which seemed to be vaguely similar to holdent-chumps.

"Holdent-Chumps," Serbinand exclaimed, "Unbelievable. No Godfried. No spaceship. No asteroids. And no bruggs. And to top it all off, my favorite food! I must be in Hallyshlosh!"

Unfortunately, Serbinand was not able to open the can as readily as against a rock. It worked. The lid parted slightly so as to compensate for its now deformed shape. He then used the metal object he found in the bag and wedged it into the crack, popping off the lid. He later discovered that this very object was designed to open such containers, but in a different way. What are the chances?

"Ahhhhhhh," he sighed as the juice ran from the can down his arm. He had swallowed most of the contents without chewing. This made him wonder why they were called baked beans when they were so cold. In his head came these words, *baked…but out cold*. Odd, but bold. Maybe they had the munchies. Soon the words turned into a tune, *Baked bean munchies. Munchies. Muncheez, cheez, cheez, cheeeeez…. Baked bean munchies!*

Serbinand did not give much more thought to that, nor to where exactly he was, how he got there, nor even what he was going to do. He just accepted the fact that he no longer was the Serbinand he knew. He no longer was confined to a ship in space, he no longer had to deal with his computer's newly annoying attitude, and he no longer was wearing the frizz-suit he grew up in. And, as a result of it all, it seemed he outmaneuvered all warrants for his detainment. Like, could anyone recognize him in this new body? Impossible. Then he thought, *well, unless they are soul family and recognize my soul....umm...but, yeah if that were to happen, that'd truly be super-vibing cool!*

That thought made him content. That was good because he intended to be in an energy that felt good. So, he was not about to let anything spoil his good mood, especially his own thoughts. Consequently, he chose to kibosh any and all fear-based thinkers. No need to hack up HAC into my own body, he reasoned. (For non-earthlings and earthlings alike, in case you don't know, HAC, in this case, refers to the stress hormones of Histamine, Adrenaline and Cortisol that the body produces as a response to repeated negative thoughts…which, as you can imagine, does wreak havoc from within causing even more unpleasant mind chatters and, yes, more hacking up of HAC…a vicious cycle—and run-on sentence—indeed.) So instead, Serbinand deliberately decided to go with the flow, live in the moment, move his body, and sport a slight smile to effectively *dose* himself with DOSE, the feel-good hormones, Dopamine, Oxytocin, Serotonin and Endorphins. And wouldn't ya know it? It actually made him feel good. And that **feeling** is what guided his actions for the rest of the day.

THE RIDICULOUS

After placing a few leftover holdent-chumps in his bellybutton for storage, Serbinand gathered the contents of his carrying case and set off through the field, hoping his legs would carry him somewhere interesting.

"What a day for a daydream—" he sang as he skipped a little, hopped a little, and did all kinds of things he was not yet able to properly do with his new-for-him body. He found himself entering a rather large area full of trees. Remembering a story he was told as a young Placellner, he recalled this sort of surrounding may be a thicket, woodland, forest, or something like that. There was a certain type of creature named Robin Hood that had made it his home. *Maybe I'll meet Robin Hood*, he hoped as he started to make his way toward the trees. *Unless, of course, he is me, and I am now he,* he reflected. *Wow, then I'd be famous. Actually, I guess I already am. This is neat.* And with that Serbinand decided there was no longer any need to go into the forest and instead turned around.

~ ~ ~

"Good morning to you, good morning to you, good morning my dearest SERRR-BI-NAAANNNN-DDDDD, good morning to youuuuuwee!!!"

"Uh—"

"Come on, up, up, up!"

"Just a few more minutes, ma—"

"Ma? Isn't that cute? He thinks I'm his mother," Godfried laughed opting to mock Serbinand. So, he continued, "and whatever happened to your voice? Do you have a beetle living in your throat?" No response. Godfried got bored and urged Serbinand on.

~ ~ ~

"Come on sleepyhead, it's time to get up. We have a big day ahead of us," Godfried continued, although he wasn't quite sure how today would be a bigger day than yesterday or the day before that, or any other day for that matter. As usual, they would fly around without any place in particular in mind—able to go wherever they wanted to go (except where they could not)—until something out of the ordinary occurred, which was rare but not as rare as not. While adventurous, it definitely lacked goals, and therefore, direction. Even so, something peculiar always did seem to happen. That's actually the theme song of the Placellner, "Placellners—young yet old, bright yet bold, small yet tall, with eyes or with a smize—peculiarly predict peculiar peculiarities parce que peculiar peculiarities peculiarly percolate to pinpoint Placellners at peculiar points, peculiarly-speaking." (As peculiarity would have it, this is repeated 1¾ times as its own peculiar chant and with its own peculiar tune).

"Placellners—young yet old, bright yet bold, small yet tall, with eyes or with a smize—peculiarly predict peculiar peculiarities parce que peculiar peculiarities peculiarly percolate to pinpoint Placellners at peculiar points, peculiarly-speaking".

Placellners—young yet old, bright yet bold, small yet tall, with eyes or with a smize—peculiarly predict peculiar peculiarities parce que peculiar peculia".

Speaking of peculiarities, of particular peculiarity, there was once a period of almost two full monthyears when nothing peculiar happened. Absolutely nothing. That all changed when Godfried bounced off the Blorsherk's Battleship while playing musical chairs. Nonetheless, the Blorsherks were not impressed to say the least. Nor did they accept Godfried's apology, despite the homemade bruggs he offered as a truce. That may have angered them even more, a more than likely probability. If you weren't aware—which Godfried pretended he was not—bruggs were responsible for the drowning and downing of the entire Blorsherk empire. So, as you can imagine, his gift-proposal backfired. Big time. Yep, it sure did. True dat. It is, in fact, what got them captured.

After tossing all bruggs and bruggs-related condiments into the ethers, Meister Blorsherk hauled Serbinand down a long barren passageway into a disorganized courtroom for a trial. The charges accounted for the damage done to the ship, but mostly they focused on the delay this trial would cause in the Blorsherk's pursuit of destruction.

While this was going on, Godfried, absolutely gobsmacked about the bruggs, was way busy designing a net to recapture them. So busy that he completely forgot to plan their getaway out of this mess.

It was during this time that Meister decided Godfried was to be used for parts and Serbinand was to be bait in their next battle. A very drastic turn of events indeed. In the throes of it all, Godfried mismanaged his net and caused a massive malfunction. Rather than capturing the bruggs, it suctioned them—every single piece, including the dried-up nuggets—right into Meister's *forever flushing* mega-toilet floating machine. Devastated to witness precious bruggs disappear, Godfried had enough and decided he could no longer watch. He immediately activated the new extend-oh-arm— which he had picked up only a few weeks prior—and delicately, yet firmly, whisked Serbinand off the Catwerlak Board of Frozen Mammal Teeth to get them out of there. This move really irritated the Blorsherks. They didn't appreciate the rather large hole it left in their ship, nor the behind-the-knee tickles.

The ensuing chase only lasted about three days. It was lively, to say the least. Godfried hid in almost every conceivable place in sector 24.3222222, and treated the whole experience like the "Hide and Sometimes Seek" game they played back home. This time, just as everyone was about to give up from boredom—yes, due to the lack of *seek*—the Blorsherk's vessel exploded. Well, to be more specific, the nation they had been at war with, the Arkens, finally caught up to them...and Boom!

As you can predict, the Arkens became quite fond of Serbinand. They decided to celebrate him with gratitude for helping to pinpoint their enemies. They invited him, red carpet style, back to Arka for rest, relaxation and two full months of self-love education and body pampering.

After the Arken experience, there had only been minor disruptions to their normal course of doing, well, nothing (until something peculiar showed up). The point being, there really was no particular reason for Godfried to wake Serbinand up right then, but he did it just the same.

"Get up, get up, get up!" he gallantly called one final time. "Uh…Ok…I'm coming, jeeezzze," Jime groaned.

Godfried didn't believe him, so he activated the *Morning Emergency Sequence Arousal Program*. All of a sudden, shutters appeared out of nowhere, and bright light poured into the room. No, this was not ordinary sunlight. This sunlight came with a sugary glow that filled the chamber with so much illumination that Jime's eyes couldn't help but pop open in surprise. But just for a moment. The resulting shock encouraged them to squeeze shut again, but harder this time—which conveniently doubled as a sun shield. Jime was baffled. He opened his eyes ever so slightly to see if the light show he saw was real. It seemed it was. He didn't like this show. So Jime closed his eyes again. This time even harder in an attempt to change the channel in his mind. It didn't work.

At the same time, the ship's audio system—The EFI 4.2, or EFI for short—kicked in with the wakey-wakey clatter of the Upppawilchk Philharmonic Chaotic Orchestra. The noise resembled the sound of a bag of nails being dragged across a bumpy concrete floor, with smaller rusty nails—fingernails, that is—rubbing against a chalkboard. Yes, fingernails as back-up instruments! Jime's ears were astounded. They consulted with his now-open eyes and reacted in a similar fashion…shock. This was rather unfortunate as it became quite the perfect recipe to invite vertigo to kick itself on in.

Note to reader:

If you had a sudden chill run through your body after envisioning the fingernail scene's sound, please know that you're not alone, signed the Author (as yet another chill ran down my spine). Now let's get back to Jime's dizzy scene.

So, while Jime was dizzily debating whether or not he had gone insane for thinking he had become a character in his dream's imagination, he was blasted by a stream of water so powerful that it drove him into the wall all the way on the other side of the room. At least it was spongy.

Knowing now that spongy walls existed, he made a mental note that should he ever again charge a wall, spongy it is. His inside voice sounded like this: *spongewallrhinokickerfriend*— confusing, yes, but he knew what he meant. This was then followed by his outside voice:

"AAAHHHOOOOOOOOHHHOOOOOWWWW!" Jime yelled, keeping his hands pressed hard against his ears.

"WWHHAATTTSSSSGGOOINNNGGGGONNNNN?" he continued, attempting to yell louder than the raucous of the pandemonium.

This happened in about as much time as an earth-person opens their eyes and lets out a yawn after a long night's sleep. Jime clearly was denied such privileges at this moment, however. In fact, he was still shaking with utter confusion when a voice filled the room.

"Good. You are up. Did you pee yourself again?" Godfried giggled as he stared at Serbinand's body crouched in the corner of his chamber, soaking in a pool of wet.

"What? Why did you do that? What's with the water? Wait a minute, ahh…Where am I? Never mind. Don't tell me," Jime squealed, then thought out loud, "This is still that crazy dream I was having. I am stuck in my imagination. That must be it. Good, I'll go back to sleep and everything will be fine when I wake up. I'll just close my eyes and delve right back into whatever imaginary concoction my masterful mind has invented and reverse out of it. Say, do you know where I can find the bed? I was just on it."

"You'll be sorry if you do that."

"What are ya talking about…Actually, who's talking? And where are you?" By now Jime wasn't so sure

he was dreaming.

"Poor Placellner, must have hit his head pretty hard when the water jet jetted you jet-style away from your bed. Doesn't explain your messed-up voice though," Godfried mused. "Now listen here, Serbinand, it's time to get up, and if you don't get up, I'll have to use the USSDWUP."

"The what?"

"The USSDWUP. You know the Ultra-Sensitive, Sometimes Dangerous, Wake Up Program." The USSDWUP is an invention Godfried invented all on his ownsome, or so he bragged. The USSDWUP temporarily converts normal matter into energy, then beams the energy to a target of its choice and—wham-bam, thank you man—restores it into its original structure. Ironically, this process—albeit without fusion—is similar to a process adopted by an Earth series that takes place in outer space, go figure. Those Earthlings musta tapped into my universal consciousness," Godfried ascertained. (He was sure his invention came first.) What he referred to as the USSDWUP, Star Trek pegged as The Transporter.

Dream or no dream, Jime realized that he wasn't up for the USSDWUP, so he decided to heed the voice and wake himself on up. Besides, he was no longer tired after what his body had just gone through.

"Fine, I'm getting up." He spoke reluctantly, and very confused, because he wasn't sure if he was just speaking to himself. Not that speaking to himself was weird, except this time he thought there was someone who wasn't actually him talking back.

"I'd feel a whole lot better if I knew what was going on," Jime voiced out loud, and then remembered he needed to know more than that, "And while you're at it, state who you are and remind me of who I am and what I'm doing here since I...."

"Listen Serbinand," Godfried interrupted. He knew this was Serbinand's way of trying to get even with him for the night before, but it wasn't going to work. *Ya right, as if pretending not to know me is going to make me feel bad or something,* Godfried thought, realizing he did feel bad, somewhat. "Look, I'm sort of sorry about last night, so if you're trying to get me back, it already worked. So just forget it."

"I really don't know what you're talking about," Jime repeated in a haze of intrigued confusion. It's times like these when he wished he had never fantasized so much about other dimensions. Maybe school could have been more interesting had he chosen to listen. But he hadn't, and that wouldn't change things at this moment anyway.

~ 74 ~

THE RIDICULOUS

So, he decided the only way to deal with the situation was to accept the fact that he had gone completely and utterly insane—and maybe even embrace it.

"Just for the sake of humor, and because I am quite fond of that outstanding perplexed look you've put on your face, I'll reward you for good acting and tell you whatever you want to know," Godfried agreed, starting at the beginning. "Your name is Serbinand Grambelfether Diddlewoppehl. You were born on Gressly-12 at precisely four in the morning at Llloperwadssl Memorial in Drancowle while your parents were on vacation. Your home planet is Placellner, where you lived a relatively uneventful life. You left home in a beautiful ship—that's me—without permission. I was given to you by your really exuberant grandmafa. We have been careening around various galaxies for what seems like an eternity. All to get away from some kind of marriage arrangement your father had made. Since then, we have basically been doing nothing aside from a little bit of exploring and ignoring, crashing and trashing, adventuring and misadventuring. Tadaaaaaaa—and that answers all your questions. Are you happy now?"

While Godfried was explaining Serbinand's life story, Jime looked around the room trying to locate where the voice was coming from. He had no luck. In fact, he was not able to see anything clearly yet. Those lights were bright!

Whatever. This was either the most realistic dream he had ever had, or something else was going on beyond his current comprehension. Sure, he'd thought about escaping from home and zooming through the universe plenty of times before, but *this can't be real, can it?* he thought. Yet here he was. And that's when he decided he may as well make the most of it and playfully play. Or at least try to. *I'm doing it. Embracing it fully. Going all in,* he smartly decided. *This is going to be fun!*

"Happy I am. Happy are you? Happy is who? Yes, who are you?" Jime responded to Godfried in non-rhythmic rhyme.

"My name is Godfried. Your computer chip friend, the Supreme Ruler of this ship, and commander of your very existence...."

"Get real."

"I am real. As real as real is real." Godfried snickered. "Now, are we finished with our little charades party? I have grown tired of this game."

"I...umm...I guesssss so. But I still don't know about this.

Am I awake in my dream?"

"Look, why don't you get undressed then redressed, take a shower in between, and after you've had a chance to shake dry, let's talk. Ok?"

No response. Serbinand, who we know is Jime (wink-wink) was speechless.

"OK" Godfried truly was getting bored. "I hereby declare a truce. Well, at least for an hour or so. You are acting way too wackadoo for this to be fun!"

~ ~ ~

"A truce…truth? If so, sounds good to me. I may even wake up from this crazy dream."

"Wake up? You mean you better not fall asleep, 'cause you know what will happen if you do."

"Yea, yea, yea, you'll blast me with the USSDWUP or whatever you call it."

"Wow, amazing, you're catching on!"

"One last question, have you seen Orville?"

"Who?"

Jime thought this matter over for a moment or two. The way things seemed to be going, anything he said was bringing him deeper into a holy shiznit pit. He decided to just let everything slide until he could make sense of it all. *Have fun, play dumb*, something inside him kept shrieking. Of all the possible actions to take right now, playing dumb did seem to be the best bet.

"Never mind, never heard of him me'self" Jime responded, walking out of the room with the hope that his legs would walk themselves to the shower, because he had no idea where he was going.

~ ~ ~

Orville returned from his excursion around the same time that Serbinand, now in Jime's body, was testing out his new physique. *What's gotten into him? Him being Jime. Jime, Jime, Jime. Jime is himmmm,* Orville thought.

"WOOOOOWWWWWWWWHHHHHEEEEEEEEE."

Serbinand whistled as he sprang from foot to foot, hobbling through the field.

Orville tried to speak to his friend, but his sing-songy tune was drowned out by a can of beans being thrown repeatedly at a rock. Orville watched in fascination as Jime picked up the can, smashed it into the boulder, danced over to where it rested, picked it up again, and resumed that same task over and over. *Ah, Jime is finding his inner caveman again*, Orville rationalized, even though that had never happened before. The process was endless, and the noises coming from Jime's mouth were quite exhausting to hear.

BANNNNNNNGGGGGGGGGGGGGGGG!
BANNNNNNNGGGGGGGGGGGGGGGG!
BANNNNNNNGGGGGGGGGGGGGGGG!

After it seemed like the noise would never end, Orville watched in shock as Serbinand then pulled a can opener out of the bag and used it to *pry* open the deformed can's partially opened lid...the wrong way.

"What's going on with you, have you gots da flu?" he chirped.

"Uhhh?" Serbinand looked around. Finding no sign of the sound, he went back to his beans.

"Did you leave your mind behind? Ignoring me is not kind. This is not the way for us to unwind!" Orville belted out exasperated lyrics.

Serbinand seemed unaware of the bird's chattering. He really couldn't hear much else above his own mouth noises. *He looked so happy now eating all his chow*, Orville thought. It truly seemed as if he hadn't eaten in days.

Of course, that is not true. We all remember his *Toblerone* feast…and he did nibble on that bark earlier, which he wished he hadn't. But this, this was really good. It tasted divine. So, nothing was going to disturb him from devouring the contents of the can. Well, except his belly button.

Just when the budgie thought he had seen everything, Serbinand stuck baked bean remnants into his navel and then walked away.

"Yelp…get some help! You're acting uncanny. You may need a nanny. Or…just go to sleep. I won't singggg a peeeeeeep." Orville sang. "Well maybe a peep-peep-peh-peeeeeeep," he reconsidered, but his jingle-attempt went unheard and Serbinand carried on his way. Despite feeling a little hurt, Orville decided that since Jime was his best friend, it was still his duty to rescue him from this bout of lunacy. Or at least watch. Especially since it was already making for good entertainment. So, he continued to monitor the soul-infused meatsuit he recognized as Jime. And that's how he spent the remainder of the day.

~ ~ ~

The first thing Jime noticed when he walked into the shower room was the mirror. Actually, it wasn't just one mirror that he saw, there were hundreds. It was as if the room exploded into mirrors! His image was reflected back at him hundreds of times, bouncing off the ceiling, floor and even the way back back wall. *Just like walking into a fun house*, he thought.

Jime never liked any fun house, as they had a tendency to scare him. Well, specifically the one where a spider was webbing webs from the ceiling, then fell—all legs flailing—and plopped right into his ear hole. That was a tickle he'd never want to feel tickled again. Who knew how the fun house makers even made that happen! "While some tickling is fun, some is more like tickle torture." He remembered being tickled by a friend's uncle's gardener's crew member's older brother. "Uninvited tickles that are too long, too hard, too deep...that's tickle torture. You sneak into a body crevice and tickle it super gently—and you're a spider—that's tickle torture too," he decided. *Why were these houses even called "fun"*, he wondered.

~ ~ ~

While normally, carnival mirrors distort reality, the mirrors in this room did not. Here the mirrors were telling the truth. "Gasp!" He gasped while saying the word gasp. (That's how he thought it was done.) He then followed up his gasping gasp with a few suppressed giggles. One came out as a burp. Jime then let out an array of words so scattered that even if they were said together in a coherent sentence, they would still have no meaning at all. After breathing himself down from this outburst, he decided there were three options open to him:

1. Get back to sleep somehow, set the intention to dream of being back home, and make that magic happen.
2. Make a run for it and hope for the best.
3. Assume the fetal position and cry until Orville—or his beloved mommy who he now misses soooo much—came to get him.

Going back to sleep meant the possibility of another wake-up subjected to the USSDWUP, or some other strange experience. Not worth the risk, likely. The fetal position, although a good idea in concept, may not work in this type of body. So, his only choice was to run. But first he had to locate the exit. Jime spun around hoping to leave through the door in which he came, but he spun with such incredible gusto that his spin overshot the door by three times. Needless to say, the dizziness that ensued nearly cost him his balance. That is, until he saw his reflection ricocheting off many walls. At that point he became disoriented and forgot where the door truly was. So instead of exiting, he fainted, and instead of running, his new body was thrust down on the plastic-glass bricked floor. (Wait...what?)

~ ~ ~

"MMMMMMMMOOOOOOOOOOOOOOOOOOO."

"Huh?"

"MMMMMMMMOOOOOOOOOOOOOOOOOOO."

"Say wha'?!" Serbinand repeated, staring at the animal standing in front of him. He couldn't believe its behavior! Chewing incessantly without any regard for manners whatsoever! Spittle flying all over the place, munching noises bellowing from its mouth hole and sloshing sounds coming from almost every orifice. And, whoa...was it actually swallowing its food only to upchuck it up and chew it all over again? *What's with that?* Serbinand wondered. He watched closer. He watched as the creature took a bite and chewed just enough to moisten the food. Clearly, *Planta Intelligentisia* would say this is not yet liquified and needed more chewing, but wouldn't you know it, the being swallowed anyway. Whoa, Serbinand wanted to encourage it to chew more so as to boost its own digestive abilities, but then reasoned that maybe big animals don't get stomach aches, bloating nor skin issues like many a folk he knows. Incidentally, Serbinand noticed in shock, the food

came—the same food, but different—softer and in small balls. *They must have a restaurant down there*, Serbinand reasoned, then watched in awe. *This beast sure liked the chef's handywork,* he thought as the animal continued to chew continuously—actually it re-chewed what was already chewed, continuously. Just chewing and chewing and re-chewing its chews. Fascinating.

~   ~   ~

"Ehh, hello," Serbinand tried, "I see you did get the memo from *Planta Intelligentisia.* I must say I am duly impressed with how well you mindfully chew." He did not get the slightest response. So instead, Orville, who is truly a smart bird, joined in to cheer the cow on, "Liquify your food! Improve your mood. To well nourish you, you must enjoy each chew. Focus on taste, temperature and texture to name a few. Roll your chow around your tongue, find the flavours…have some fun. Whatever you do, just chew, chew, chew, chewwwww." Still nothing.

~   ~   ~

Serbinand who was unable to understand the bird, was unimpressed and ready to give up. That is, until he had an idea. "MMMMMOOOOOOOO," he uttered, despite not knowing its meaning.

To this, the cow stopped chewing, and stared straight at him as if to say, *Hey. That's my language you're speaking. What's going on!?* Aside from that, there was no other reaction.

Serbinand continued with that approach. It was working, so why not go all in. He bent down to the ground, got on all fours, dug his head into the grass, and began to chew. *Not bad*, he thought. "Pretty good, actually," he burst out with great delight.

"MMMMMMMMMMMMOOOOOOOOOOOOO!", he uttered

again, this time with both force and pride. And to think I have been walking on this chew-haven food, since I got here. What a planet!"

The cow was really not quite sure what was going on, but as long as this creature did not interfere with its job of eating, everything would be alright. A cow's career objectives were very simple: *Eat. All. The. Grass.* That was it. Very direct. This particular cow had it all figured out years ago, as a calf. *Once I'm finished with this spot, I'll move onto that one. And then after that, I'll move over there.* She really was independent as a cow. Even left the farm before her parents gave the official okay. Ever since, she has been passionate about fulfilling her grass-eating goals. She would let nothing interfere. Never had there even been an issue either. Until now.

A human was standing directly on top of the next edible spot, a slight imperfection with the plan. Well, this was troubling. What to do? Only one solution came to mind. *Kick the human.* Yes, that would be easy to do. And without missing a beat in her chew-venture, she let out a slightly louder bellow of a

"MMMMMMOOOOOOO" and deftly booted Serbinand in the chest, sending him flying. He landed meters away, out cold.

~ ~ ~

Godfried, observing Jime lying on the bathroom floor, decided it was time for the USSDWUP again. This time in psychedelic mode.

"This is going to be so much fuuunnnnnnn!" he chanted.

~ ~ ~

Serbinand woke to the sight of that same tiny yellow creature hovering in the air. It was staring directly at him.

"Whaaadda ya want little yellow fellow?" he grumbled through his groggy state. He got no response. Little yellow just carried on looking at him seemingly dumbfounded, which we all know he was.

"What in the flotinkin is going on? Okay, now I want answers. Where am I, what am I looking at, and why am I talking to myself?

Godfried are you around?" Serbinand wondered out loud. With no audible answer, and after many moments of silence, Serbinand began to remember tidbits of odd experiences he had experienced over the course of the day. Probably the longest day ever. This is how he remembered it:

Godfried was not much fun to travel with. I said a prayer for him in silence. But first I put my mind to my heartspace to ensure I felt good. Then I suggested that the energies of the universe guide him to unwind and find his fun. Said my affirmations. Got into bed, belly empty. Dozed off. A strange explosion of energy dazzled me out of sleep. I heard myself

~ 84 ~

THE RIDICULOUS

think "is that a light show on steroids?!" It was so odd. Next thing I know, I was fully clothed—standing—in what appears to be the mythical Earth School—the planet where trees grow, and where unbeknownst to most of its inhabitants, you feel most fulfilled by bettering your being, mastering your mind, raising your frequency, and ultimately falling in love with yourself. So, at first, I was thrilled. Then I felt frustrated because I saw no welcome sign. Unless I missed it, of course, which is possible, I guess. I mean I wasn't on the lookout. I didn't even think about it. All I wanted was food. Found me a chewing champion. Ate some great yum-yums together with it. Discovered the moo-moo sure was impressive not just as a chewer, but as a kicker too. She helped me land a figure-eight midair! Then with zero to no applause, no snickers, jeers nor comments, I realized Godfried truly was not around. Godfried not around? Hmmm. I don't get it, though. I just don't get it. And... YaAY!!!! How amazingly awesome is that!!! Serbinand thought.

Other than utter confusion, Serbinand had no critical complaints. He was, in fact, enjoying himself, despite the slight injuries along the way. Things may be better though if he could figure out where he was, who he should meet and what he was there to do. After several minutes of deliberate deliberation with himself, he decided that he was not, could not, and would not be able to answer those questions. So, he resolved to make the best of the situation, and continued on his way to nowhere, being sure to avoid standing in the path of any animal that ate grass.

~ ~ ~

Jime was zapped with a laser beam. He was broken down into approximately 7,999,788.662 pieces, which, as one might expect, was not gratifying in any way. He was sent hurling through the air, in the format of particles, into a long cold compression tube. The shaft was about the size of a toothbrush container, which could easily double as a convenient storage compartment. Once inside, Jime's body was shaken for nearly twelve minutes. After the dizzying process was over, the contents of the tube—umm Jime (dressed in Serbinand's

frizz-suit and now represented as particles)—was dumped on the floor. Dust was everywhere. Splashes of cold water then splashed the particles, turning them into a muddy mess. A final blast of laser hit them and *Holy Shmoly Kawowzoly* suddenly the entire Jime mess merged together to create one lone Jime. Once again, Jime was whole. It was as if nothing traumatizing happened. In fact, he now stood only slightly to the left of where it all started. Only he still looked like Serbinand.

~ ~ ~

"That was the USSDWUP, I presume?" he mumbled while holding back the nausea.

"Catching on. That's great. More importantly, great awakening and good morning to you too!"

"Was that all really necessary?" "Are you awake?"

"Yea, but...."

"Then it was necessary, don't you think?" Godfried defended. "Look," Jime started, "I don't need this. I don't need you, I don't need this body costume, and I definitely do not need the USSDWUP. What I *do* need is an explanation of where I am, what this is, why I am here...and a detailed description of how to swap myself out of these costumed clothes would be nice. Fill me in and I will be a much more happy-go-lucky person, or whatever I am. Kapeesh?"

~ ~ ~

Godfried decided to ignore his friend, hoping to let this spell of lunacy dissipate.

~ ~ ~

"I asked a question! Answer me! Where are you? Hello...Ah, ummm...Are you there? Hellllowwwww. Hey...what do I need to do to get your attention...fall asleep again? Wait, just kidding...hellowww?"

CHAPTER EIGHT
REVELATIONS

"Hi...I *bet* you're wondering who I am and what I'm doing here barging into the story and all, but I think it's appropriate for me to make an appearance right about now. Geez...you look alarmed, taken aback even. Hmmm...I didn't expect that. I was, ahh, expecting cheers, applause, praise. Well...Ahh...Hmmm, this just got really embarrassing!

I guess you, I, we, can pretend this never happened, which would be a great psychological task indeed. But I really think it is in everybody's best interest to stick around and read these pages, just so I can explain myself.

But if you're not feeling it, you're not feeling it. So...go ahead and skip to the next part. That will be in the next few pages or more. Not sure yet at this point, since it has not yet been written. But be warned: If you do skip this chapter, I am sure you will miss something pretty important. Maybe.

Oh you're still here. Nice. Good choice. Welcome to something pretty important: Business. Book business, that is. This book's business to be specific. And now I will answer what you're probably wondering. I mean…you *bet*ter be wondering. (That was a joke as you may have noticed that I *bet* you in the very first sentence of this chapter. It was my way to kind of coax you along. And, by "my way" I mean belonging to me, myself and I…the…(drum roll, please)…creator of this story: Yes, *the Author*, if you will. Well, *co*-author and *co*-creator to be more specific, as I co-create with another creative who edits in elements of her own imagination too, sometimes.

Anyway, no need to be confused. This tale has not (yet?) been taken over by aliens, nor terrorists, nor even an obscure virus forcing everyone into lockdown. And no, the characters won't have to eat any bizarre food, solve a ridiculously intelligent riddle or perform a dangerous task. This is not reality TV. This is real LIFE. Well, real life imaginings…in book format, that is.

Now, what am I doing here? Very simply, I noticed that Serbinand and Jime haven't been having much luck lately. I had the opportunity to observe them for quite some time now, and often I just shake my head. *So why do it? Why continue to create a story about them?* That's something I often wondered. Even now, I am wondering the very same thing. Hmmm.

Well, to be honest, it's actually quite simple. After watching our characters struggle to understand what happened to them—you know, the transfer of Serbinand into Jime, and Jime into Serbinand—I realized their struggle was real. And struggling with this is something you, our reader, may be able to relate to in some way since our character's adventure became quite ridiculous. Right?

Wait...You agree? You listen to me. These ridiculous adventures are to be enjoyed. I know what I am talking about. As such, I think I would know the proper direction for the characters to take. I am The Author after all. I can do with them as I please. Even if I don't say please. Or even think it.

Oops...wow. My my. I apologize. I don't know what happened there. I didn't write that last part. That wasn't really me. I don't believe it was anyway. That must have been Godfried's new personality coming out through me. I sincerely apologize for that. Yes, I like to act out all my characters before writing them in. It's the way they audition. Sometimes it gets confusing though. I never know whose thoughts will be revealed when I open my mouth. Quite the fun surprise, actually, but only at times.

Any hoodley doodley, let me get back to my point, as well as the story at hand! If you are struggling reading this adventure because it may seem *ridiculous*, I will give you the Coles Notes, Cliff Notes and SparksNotes versions all in one. So...where it stands is that Godfried now thinks "Serbinand"—who we all know is Jime—is desperately trying to get even with him once and for all. He rationalized that Serbinand must have really hated being the butt of practical jokes, especially the harmful ones — AND — as such, chose to get revenge by playing dumb— even if it meant accepting all forms of pain (which only ever occurs when one's subconscious mind reigns supreme—something that everyone and anyone should, and could, course correct).

Meanwhile, the real Serbinand—the one in Jime's body—seemed quite content, despite feeling the effects of gravity (with no real warning sign).

Orville, on the other hand, plainly believes his very best friend has gone berserk—completely bonkers. And yet he was still enjoying it. Who can blame him? It's not every day a transfer of souls happens.

Jime, though, well he seemed to be in the most distress. While he should be self-impressed that he made his escape dreams come true, it seems he did not enjoy escaping into a reality of pain. And he didn't have a *once-escaped* escape plan, so he couldn't quite escape what he escaped into.

Now, I know this still does not really explain why I halted everything to make an appearance. Nor does it explain why I am going to halt this halt. Just suffice it to say I need a bathroom break. Until then, use this as your cue to drink some water (the energized kind), eat a fresh fruit (they're all high vibrational), and then open your mind to what is about to unfold.

~ ~ ~

Ok I am back. I'm now ready to let you know why I so suddenly interrupted my own fable.

So…it turns out that although my co-author and I thought it would be neat to make Jime and Serbinand switch bodies, we hadn't really contemplated what would happen after they did *exactly* that. I mean, we still have NO IDEA how they are going to adjust to their new circumstances. To put it bluntly, we had been left in a rather precarious situation. Actually, *we* weren't, *our characters were.*

So, I decided to invite all of them back to my house. I figured we could sit down together and hash this all out. Of course, I do realize there might be a great deal of hostility and confusion, rather

THE RIDICULOUS

than downright jubilation, but what has to be done just has to be done, right?

Oh, I almost forgot. You, dear reader, are invited too. Come along now...."

~ ~ ~

In a small, rather cluttered, and now crowded room, Serbinand, Jime, Orville and Godfried—who was present in the form of a mobile extension unit—sat around a medium-sized desk, oak. Each appeared to be out of sorts. Yes, they were distressed and befuddled. Behind a desk, with fingers punching away at the keyboard (writing these very words), sat an Author...ME! (*Hi there!*)

On either side of my fancy expensive computer were piles of paper, along with paper clips, a stapler, a staple remover, and various other unmentionable items. Beside the desk was an overflowing garbage bin and a small refrigerator, which usually housed a sandwich or two, a green shake, and a small tub of orange peels—hand painted. Across the room sat a fake plant and a yellowed telephone. This has no bearing to the story, although they do seem to have developed quite the attachment for each other and have stayed together since the day they met. A fairly large futon was situated on the back wall behind the desk where this Author—**yes, that's ME**—has had the occasional rest between paragraphs. The surprising thing about a futon is that it is both a couch and a bed. It can be transformed at any point just by pulling on it. Sometimes, if you get really lucky—or unlucky, depending on your position at the time—it morphs while you are on it! It is actually my belief that the futon has a different purpose altogether which the government will share with us one day. A miscellaneous assortment of crackers and pizza crusts were spread throughout the room, including on the futon. Where there were none, often there were crumbs.

"Welcome. I have invited you here to this cozy office to dispel the confusion you've been experiencing for the last day or two. Let's get to the bottom of this," I spoke.

"Wait just a sec here, ah…umm…hmm…Let's see, how should I put this? Ok…Ummm. Who are you, where are we, and why do I see me sitting across from me? And…whose eyes am I looking out from? Whose voice is speaking my words?" Jime asked, clearly discombobulated.

"Yeah, exactly. And what are we doing here?" Serbinand added.

"Well, I created all of you. You are all characters in my book.

And I brought you here."

"It is not conceivably possible that you created my existence. I am Godfried," Godfried's portable unit interjected. "If anything, I created your existence…and his, and his and that flying thing's too."

"Here we go again. Godfried *the great* has spoken," Serbinand muttered under his breath.

"I don't believe a word," Jime uttered, "nor do I really know what is going on for that matter. Here I am looking at someone who resembles the *me* I've seen in the mirror for years—and I see that very same *someone* is looking at who I think is *me* who actually looks *unlike* me and more like a *mishmash*. Jime suddenly felt defeated, "Like who is thinking my head's thoughts? That mashup or me?"

~ 94 ~

Feeling the need to console his characters, Author interjected, "Well, in good news, you're all alive." But then he saw Jime roll his eyes. This threw him off, made him feel defensive so he got defensive and abruptly added, "but only within MY story."

"Yea, right. Sure," Jime chortled.

"Hey, hey, hey, hey, hey! Don't be mouthing off to me, Jime. I created each and every one of you. And I can uncreate you too. So, if I were you, I would be very careful about how you act around here. Otherwise, I may just write you out of your very own story."

"Oho! Listen to Mr. Almighty and Powerful!" Godfried exclaimed.

"True, this is ludicrous. It can't be possible," Serbinand agreed, almost too stunned to take offense, yet clearly agitated.

Sensing tension amidst all the confusion, Orville decided to humor everyone instead, and began flying upside down while busting out in song. In his best soprano voice (which wasn't going to win him any golden tickets), he sang "Yeah, riiiight. Author sir, you seem so bright…nottttt. But oh, what a great plottttt. Clearly, we are in the wrong spot.

"Wrong spot? This is fascinating." Serbinand got sidetracked, "You're a bird that can talk." Orville, bewildered to be heard, was actually starting to like this. "And here I thought Jime went insane, but who am I to complain? I'm outside my house, more free than a mouse, getting entertained all the sammmmme."

Hearing a bird sing as though it was auditioning for *American Idol* did nothing to unconfuse them. It actually confused them even more.

Seeing their bewildered faces, Orville smiled with delight. "Well, that was swell, I could kvell," he stated, clearly happy having come to the realization that now there were even more *beings* he could communicate with.

~ ~ ~

In that instant Jime had a sudden realization that found its way out of his mouth almost as quickly as it entered his awareness. With an air of confidence, he spoke, "Just a moment, everyone. Just wait one sec, Mr. Author, if that is your *real* title. If you created us, as you say you did, and you write everything that we do and say, then how come we are able to say all that we've said, which is clearly something you didn't want to hear? Huh, huh, huh? Does having this discussion with us more precisely mean you're speaking to yourself, through yourself, telling yourself not to not agree with yourself?"

"What?" everyone wondered aloud.

"A ponderance indeed…Metaphysically, psychologically, philosophically, ethically, non-logically, and, yes, even musicalllllllly," sang Orville.

"Yes. Exactly that, Orville" Jime agreed, and added "I mean, are you delusional, Author sir, or are we? Like, what is really going on here? Actually, whatever it is, I don't like it," Jime let out an outbreathed puff, seemingly stumped.

"Look guys, I don't like this anymore than you do. In fact, it has given me the creeps to have you all sitting here in my home office. I mean, clearly you are outside the pages of my book at the moment. And it seems you almost have a life of your own. Consequently, I would really like to resolve this. ASAP. I have your trilogy to write. So, if y'all don't mind," Author pleaded.

"Don't mind? Ha!" Serbinand spoke, "Why don't you start by telling us what's really going on and how we can resolve it."

"Finally. It's nice to have your attention," Author exclaimed with jubilation, "Okay. Serbinand. You are now Jime. And Jime. You are now Serbinand. And there you have it!"

"What?" Both Serbinand and Jime squawked. "You've switched bodies." Author clarified.

"Why'd you do that to us?" All of them asked, not quite in unison at all.

"Well, you each seemed pretty uninspired in the world I invented you into. So, something had to be done. I knew I needed to create a change. You each were wanting some otherworldly adventure. So why not help make that happen for you? And upon having that realization, a huge explosion went off without a hitch on some far-off subsection of some galaxy that may or may not exist. The impact was felt nowhere and by no one other than you and you." Author pointed to Jime and Serbinand, "And that's why, and how, you switched bodies, and why your original body now has a new soul. You are similar to a *walk-in* so to say"

"A walk-in? Really?" Serbinand asked in amazement.

"This is kinda ridiculous" Jime proclaimed, "but without the *kinda*. This is definitely ridiculous."

~ ~ ~

"Exactly, Serbinand, I mean Jime, no—I mean Serbinand," Author piped in, and added under his breath, "Wow, this is confusing even for me…" then admitted, "but you are right, you nailed it—your adventures have been ridiculous. And that's because you're not real. So, are you willing to accept that now?" he asked.

"I don't know what to accept. I don't know what to believe," Jime responded.

"What if we just want to get out of your office? Would you put us back in the book and let us adventure in the body we each are accustomed to?" Serbinand asked.

"Nope," Author said.

"Nope? Why *nope?*" demanded Jime, intending to change Author's mind.

"You are nothing without me. You are in no position to influence me on what to do. I'm not changing a thing. The purpose of this get-together was to let you know what occurred, not to give you a choi—"

"We'll go on strike!" Godfried interjected with ferocity.

"Yea!" Serbinand joined in, agreeing with Godfried for the first time in weeks.

"Sure, why not?" Jime accepted.

"You can't do that," Author laughed, but wondered…*could they?*

"Why nottttt? Why nohhhtttt? Why noougggghhhhttt" Orville sang those words on repeat for no less than 39 seconds.

"Why nohttttttttttttt -ttttt -tttt -ttttt!"

Finally, Author interjected. (He just couldn't take the tune anymore.) With a sincere, yet adamant tone, he replied "Because you are *my* characters, in *my* story. That's why! Are you forgetting that? You do what I say you do."

"I think you are missing something fairly important here, King Author," Godfried mocked, "You brought us out of the book. You made us real. So now we are. Thanks for that, by the way. And as such I propose that we claim our independence and go on our own merry ways. You can't really do anything to stop us."

"But you are my characters, I created you! You can't do this to me. After what I've done for you all!"

~ ~ ~

"All you've done for us? Now I must fuss. Sure…you allowed me to be free. But what am I without he…or he?" Orville sneered out a tune while hovering between Jim and Serbinand, clearly still confused.

"You've got a point. Come on all y'all. Orville too. Let's go," Jime said, "We can do better than this. I'm actually excited to talk it through and see what we come up with."

"Stay. Let's just sit back on down. We can work this out. Hey, we can even order pizza!" Author seemed to plead, "Pizza. Real pizza. None of you will be sorry."

"No!" Godfried shouted.

"Not gonna happen," Serbinand agreed.

"But wait, mate. Let's reconsider our fate, mate. Because pizza in your tum tum spells out 'yum yum,'" piped up Orville.

"Big nope from me too, and I love pizza." declared Jime in quite the huff.

Orville, beside himself with delight (still relishing in the fact that all these characters—real or not—can each hear him), busted out a lovely little ditty, "Do not dwell my friends. No need to yell my friends. All is well my friends. We'll just rebel my friends. This is swell my friends. Time to excel my friends." And with that, Orville's ditty was done.

Silence.

Serbinand broke it and drawled out the obvious, "How now, pal?" Orville, thrilled to be in the spotlight, continued, "How is WoW. We just ka-PoW. And bid dear Author a sweet farewell... And then he belted out what he seemed to think was a chorus, "Fair well, dear Author, as we bid you farewell. Is that fair? Well, yeah it's fair...Farewell."

"Come on, everyone. Let's get out of here." Jime agreed, "Let's go for a drink together—with no Author—and work this out between us somehow." With that declaration they all got up and left the office, singing the ditty together, "Fair WELLL dear Author as we bid you farewell. Is that fair? Well...Yeah it's fair...Well...FAREWELLLLLLL!!!!." Even Godfried joined in, as it was quite the catchy tune.

~ ~ ~

"Hi. Me again! Well, it looks like I messed up a little bit, so I am going to hafta figure something out. This truly is embarrassing. In the meantime, the story is going to take a slight *pause* until I, err, *we, yes WE*...no, I mean I...umm...WE.... Geez, why can I not say what I want to say?! I am not sure what's happening. Who is in control here? Whatever the case, this has to get resolved. So dear reader, please chillax, settle down, go into your special space.

Maybe get some baked beans, if you like them like Jime does, and chew slower than you've ever chewed before. I should have everything back to normal soon. No more than a few pages, I hope...or 100 plus chews.

CHAPTER NINE

CHARACTERS WITHOUT AN AUTHOR

After that uncanny exchange of words at Author's office, Serbinand, Jime, Orville, and Godfried abruptly left. They found themselves entering the *Inky Dinky Schnitzel House Pub & Brewery* just across the street. Yes, they did look like an unusual bunch, but with society's new emphasis on the 'be true to you' campaign, almost everyone's appearance these days had been quite unique. If for some obscure reason they looked perfectly "normal", perhaps then they would look strange. So, why not go for being *odd* and just blend in. And that's what they did! To put it simply, no one paid them much attention. The cars kept moving at their regular speed, the pedestrians minded their own business—busy on their phones, and the bar-staff saw nothing out of the ordinary. Plus, they were the only ones there. Perfect!

Even so, they chose to sit near the back of the restaurant. The table was round. It had wood shavings peeling off, and parts of it were held with tape. A spongy leather couch softened with age wrapped around the table in a half-moon shape. It's there where they chatted amongst themselves for the very first time.

Still beside himself with delight, Orville belted out "I love this new life, despite the current strife. Thank you Author sir and madam for making me free. Golly geee…I can finally be me." Orville glanced around and noticed the crew of them made up a whole audience. This inspired him greatly. "Now that folks finally understand, I think I may start a band." Then he curtsied.

"I don't know how I feel about that—and all this," Jime answered with a slight smirk, then reiterated what he had previously iterated, "It just seems kinda weird, you know, thinkin' the way I normally think but then remembering I am not the me I knew me as before. Then seeing the *me* I knew me as before sitting across from some new me, speaking with me as though I am not me, even though I still feel like I am me, but there's no way I am me. I know because of my meatsuit…. Touch me, it's frizzy. It's all so mind-boggling too. Like what really makes me *me*? My mind? My body?" As you can see, Jime was feeling completely uncertain what all this meant for his heart and spirit. He continued, "AND…to top it off, if what Author says is true, maybe the thoughts I thought that I thought *aren't* actually my thoughts, but his…Hmm." Now he sounded bewildered.

"Well, I've always thought for myself. I know that much…and I'm quite confident I am going to be just fine on my own. I say we just break away and go along our merry way. I know I'll be happier. I have some practical jokes to practice and perfect," Godfried asserted.

Serbinand still found his *friend's* new personality to be extremely irritating. This time he spoke up, making his true feelings about Godfriend obvious to the others too, "Practical jokes are neither

~ 104 ~

practical nor a joke. Yours hurt. Yes, they hurt me. You hurt me. Now that you know, you could care!" *That felt soooo good*, he thought, *I guess I'm already finding my roarrr, and I was just on earth for like a millisecond or more.*

Just as he was getting carried away in his thoughts, he heard Godfried speak. "HEY!" exclaimed Godfried. Before Godfried could continue, Orville had a sort of an "Aha" and flew forward to share, "Hold a minute. We can win it. Slow it down! Reverse the frown. We are finally without that clown!" Orville was in his element. "When (now) do you think is time (now) to figure out what to allow, what to fix and what to nix?

"I dunno...as soon as we can, I suppose," chimed in Serbinand.

The answer is now. N o w. NOWWWWWWWW la la la laaaaah nohhwww ow owwww… dooodooodooodooodooo dooo…. Kapowww!!!"

"Hey, who made you king, birdbrain?" Godfried muttered, smirking at the irony.

And with that, Jime also had enough of Godfried and directed his next sentiment to him, "You! So, you're just a computer chip who babbles? Wow. I am so done with you, and I barely even met you. Practical jokes aren't always funny. And I know firsthand that yours likely *never* are. Your practical jokes seem to be hurtful—both to the body and the mind, no matter whose mind is in whose body. So, you gotta stop. No one wants them." Then he added, "And, watch how you talk to my little friend. Take this as my warning. You have been warned."

"Wait. What did he…it, well, my ship's computer chip, do to you?" Serbinand inquired, suddenly missing the old Godfried.

"You really want to know? I'll tell ya. *The Emergency Arousal Sequence Program* thingamajiggy, or whatever you call it. Yep, it was activated! And if that wasn't enough—which it was—after I passed out in the bathroom of mirrors, he also enacted the USSDWUP." Jime exclaimed.

"No!"

"Yup."

"He never even attempted that on *me*!"

"I thought it was you, so you better just watch yourself," Godfried interjected.

"SHUSH-UP!" Serbinand and Jime chimed in almost-unison.

Then Serbinand looked back at his previous body and encouraged its new owner to continue. "Omgosh, that's crazy. What was it like?" Serbinand asked, curious yet slightly amused.

"Crazy for sure. Now how do I explain it?! Let's see. Well, he broke me…or you…errr, or, umm, us…? Whatever, I guess that's not the point. So yeah, just imagine being broken, and being aware that you're being broken. Yep, broken into a million pieces, that is. Sorry, I mean 7,999,788.662 pieces, as *Mister Majesty* proclaimed. Then picture being hurled—in little bits—through the air, scattering all around only to land in some kind of jar. Yes, a jar. Well, I guess it's more of a blender. Yes, a blender. A blender that mixes you up much like how a bartender would mix a drink. Only this time you *are* the drink. A pulpy one."

"Ouch! That does not sound like fun! Nor a drink I would ever want to drink." Serbinand seemed astounded yet relieved it wasn't him in his body at the time.

"Well, you wouldn't even have had time to drink it, err, me," Jime proclaimed, "Just as I thought I was resigned to being swallowed, I then got plunged into an ice bucket on a high counter that spilled. Miraculously, mid-spill and mid-air body innards and *outtards* became one, once again. And that, my friend (or foe, I'm not sure yet), gave me just enough time to land with a thud."

"THUDDDDD ddddd!" Godfried added, for effect.

"Wait, don't hate. I can't relate. Focus on love. Be a dove." chirped Orville, seeming defeated.

"What?" one of the three of them asked, just after the other two inwardly questioned it.

"Truth is, I've heard enough unpleasant banter. I would rather motivate and be your stand-in cantor." Clearly Orville became intent on pursuing his passion. "Or maybe I'm just voracious.... Perhaps we need to eat food, then we'll feel gracious," sang Orville patiently while losing patience.

"True dat," and on that note Jime summoned the waitress over. They ordered candy-covered insects (those were for Orville), a plate of veggie sticks, black bean soup all around, large nachos with no cheese and no meat and no toppings, a box of crackers (also for Orville who was willing to share), round of superfood shakes to make everything more super, and the Inky Dinky Schnitzel House house special schnitzel....

Godfried, who perhaps actually took the banter between Jime and Serbinand to heart, if that's even possible, spoke up, but this time in a kinder tone, "Ok, I think the little yellow rhyming fellow over here had a point. Let's work towards figuring this out, starting with why you guys decided to switch places. There must be a logical reason and I'm sure it wasn't due to some *undetected* explosion or because our Author *pal* chose to make it happen. So, what truly occurred? What do you believe?" Godfried seemed intrigued.

Jime began, "All's I know is that I was walking in a field with Orville hoping to discover a new adventure on a different planet. The next thing I know, I'm dressed in a creature suit that doesn't zip up nor come off, leading me to believe that I was that creature. A creature who slept in an extra comfy big bed, mind ya. A creature goaded by *you*—who I now know is, umm, just a computer, *who*—errr, I mean *that*—thinks he's the supreme ruler of the universe or something along those lines."

"Go on, and on and on and on and onnnnn," urged Orville, clearly eager to hear more.

"So yeah, maybe my dreams to leave Earth weren't properly specific. I should have envisioned myself as me, rather than leave it up to someone else's imagination," Jime shared this thought while tilting his head in amazement, recognizing that he was actually beginning to believe the Author dude in some unfathomable way.

By now Serbinand was eager to interject. "Imagination or not, I am you. But still me. As you. Being me...Learning how to be you...so I can work your *being*...as me," he philosophized.

~ 108 ~

Then, realizing just how comedic this whole thing would be if it were to become an actual book or movie, he chuckled, "I experienced something similar, but in reverse. One moment I am trying to get away from you-know-who over there. The next thing I know, I'm standing in a field, likely the very one you were just talking about, but in a different body—yours, apparently—and with a type of gravity that actually makes you stick to the ground or fall towards it if you are kicked!"

"That surely explains why Jime became so odd! I finally get that it was you in his bod," Orville piped in.

"Wait!" Jime piped up, suddenly concerned, "What was he doing to my body?"

"Well," Serbinand interjected, laughing, "I was just testing out its functions."

"That seems logical. Whoa...wait...all?!" Jime questioned suddenly getting a visual of a scene that now he couldn't unsee...of himself. Wild.

"Well, I got as far as the cubby-hole for holdent-chumps—I mean, *baked beans* in your speak." Serbinand said matter of factly. Before Jime could even attempt to visualize what a cubby-hold for baked beans could possibly mean, Serbinand tried to reassure him, "Don't worry. Everything seems to be in working order now, alright? Pretty sore all over...but I feel freeeeee. Your life is a whole lotta fun, according to meee!" Clearly Orville's way with words was rubbing off.

The waitress, Lucy, arrived and placed the food on the table. She was about to walk away to stand in the distance, when Serbinand called her over. She was used to colorful personalities, even outrageous ones, but something seemed different about this crew. She wondered if this was going to be a similar hoopla like what happened two summers ago. While she was finishing her shift, an entire busload of doomsday preppers arrived. Most of them wore lavish costumes consisting of face masks and camouflaged garb to blend into the decor of the restaurant. They had their own language, communicating by the clicking of their teeth. For some reason, they thought it was the funniest thing in the world (perhaps the entire universe), when she would say "Pardon?" or "Sorry, what did you say?". To that, they just clicked their teeth more, but in unison. This played out over and over and over and over and became a game that lasted just short of two hours. In the end, she learned a few click tones herself and got an enormous tip. Ever since, she has always clicked once during her request to take someone's order, hoping for at least one click back.

In front of her was a human accompanied by a budgie who seemed to be the leader. Beside them was a talking computer that looked like a *Star Wars* fan. It appeared to be a cross between R2D2 and C3PO with a bit of Chewbacca thrown in for laughs. Then there was one hefty guy in a surreal type of costume, with eyes that looked oh so real! She was about to ask where she could get a similar get-up but reconsidered. Last week when she asked a fella why he was wearing his hat upside down, he went absolutely bonkers! It took six people to calm him down, and one to hold his hat.

She was then forced to listen to his twelve-minute perfectly rehearsed script about the proper way to wear any headpiece, regardless of what society had to say.

So, she played it safe and decided not to say a word. But with nothing better to do—and to avoid her boss finding her something less better to do—she decided to approach them and chat them up, anyway. *There are only so many times she could polish the doorknobs, mop the misshapen tile in the basement, and rotate the mirror in each salt shaker,* she reasoned.

"Do we look normal to you?" Serbinand questioned.

"Well, you would need to define the word 'normal' for me to answer you *normally*," she answered.

"Alright. Normal in the sense that if you looked at us, you would not see anything out of the ordinary nor anything worth questioning."

"Why?" she questioned.

"Ahh, maybe I can answer that one," Godfried began. "No!" Serbinand cried.

"Why not? Let him talk. He seems intriguing. So does this frizzbally one," she exclaimed as she looked towards Jime.

"Hardly incredible. We are not real, so the spiel goes. We are characters in a story written by very well-known authors," Godfriend began.

"How do you know they're well-known?" Jime asked.

"I don't. But they created us, right? So, if they did, then they must be good. I mean, take me for example. I am soooooo intelligent...so presumably they gave this gift to me! If they are that skilled, it only follows that they must also be well-known."

"No, it doesn't. It makes you delusional and egocentric!!!" Serbinand exclaimed.

"I think not. I know what I know and that is everything. I am incredibly gifted, dear friend. I believe it and you should too. And so it is," Godfried defended.

"Here ye, here yeeeeeehh. Your majesty—well, your self- proclaimed majesty—has spoken. And so it be..." Serbinand feigned kindness, while crunching on a veggie stick.

"Simmer down. Thwart that frown. Chill out. Stop the pout", Orville interrupted with a guffaw.

Just then the waitress piped up. "Hold up. Hold on. If you want me to sit with you and listen to your adventure, all y'all better start playing nice. Otherwise, I am outta here. Yes, you do look uniquely different as do pretty much most of the folk here. Many seem just a few stitches away from a massive lobotomy, or at least where I've wanted to suggest one. So, if you have something to share or ask, then get on with it. I have no desire to listen to your rambles about something I know nothing about... And another thing, I know a lot—" Lucy seemed defensive now and started getting a little emotional in her rant. She shed a tear.

"Whooaaww, are you okay?" Jime interrupted.

"Yeah, for sure. It's just that someone once called me *out-to-lunch-Lucy* and insisted I know nothing about nothing. So when I realized there is something I know nothing about, I guess it triggered me." Lucy responded disappointed in herself that she had not yet mastered the technique to ditch her dysfunctional belief. "Crazy since I often got top marks on exams…yet still took their nonsense nonsense to heart."

"Well, why not pour yourself a beer?" Serbinand offered, as if that would help, but that's all he could think of.

Lucy, who rarely drinks, cautiously glanced at her watch, noticed her shift was about to end in three minutes and 13 seconds, and decided that it's fine to have a drink once in a while. "Okey dokey, but no beer. I'd rather go for something more healthy…Hmmm, how about we each do a shot of mezcal?" She thought aloud, "Yes, may as well do parasite control. A trick I learned in Mexico. Mezcal coming right up and it's on the house." Then off she strode.

"Whatddya' do that for?" Jime asked.

"What?" retorted Serbinand.

"You know perfectly well what I'm talking about."

"No, I don…ohh, you mean calling Lucy over, and telling her a bit too much about our situation?" Serbinand guessed.

"Ding ding ding ding ding!" Jime responded. He was clearly irked, "Yes, why would you ever entice someone else to join us?"

"Well …Jime, I have only one answer to give you, and that is '*Why not?*'" Serbinand said proudly.

"Why not? That's not an answer. That's a question. And not a good one at that." Jime was none too impressed.

"Well, I recently encountered a Sleepfuzz….. Good or no good, I now tell truths, as should we all. And that was my truth," Serbinand reflected. He was defensive, yet *truthful*.

"I have an idea," Godfried seemed inspired, "As a non-character in the so-called book, maybe we can use her to our advantage! Then we can get back to whatever it was that we were doing or wanting to do. Clear?"

"Clear as your career," piped up Orville excited to get another chance to hear his own rhyme, even if it did not truly rhyme nor make much sense.

"Crystal," groaned Jime in an upward pitch, clearly not clear on what was meant to be clarified, "And how are we going to achieve that?"

"Well, if Author refuses to accept our motion, let's get Lucy to stir things up and make a commotion," Godfried said smugly, obviously still influenced by Orville.

"Still not fully following. What do ya mean?" Jime enquired.

This time Serbinand spoke, "I get it. What Godfried means is that Author may actually listen to her. She could help us work everything out, without him terminating us from his book, also known as our life."

"That's right. If not, she can get in touch with the media and tell them our story. Or maybe she can threaten him. The possibilities are endless," Godfried brain-blissed, "Do you see what I see?"

THE RIDICULOUS

"Sorta...but likely not. Why can't we just do this ourselves?" Jime wanted to know. "Why can't we just go to Author and tell him to cut us loose from his story, or write us back in, but on our terms!? If not, we can quit, strike, cross the line or do whatever it is characters who are on the loose are able to do."

Orville believed differently. "May not be possible nor a line that's crossable. Me thinks he does have full control over you, and you, and you. You're his crew. I guess me, too. I bet his writing style is why my singing makes me smile." Orville now wanted to be a performer. He was loving this.

Apparently Jime was too. He chimed in, "I guess his imagined-up imaginings could be influencing our each and every thought...just to get more books bought. So going on strike may be exactly what he'd like. He wants us to seem ridonkulous so people look and buy his book."

Wowww, they all thought. *He's now rhyming too!*

"I'm not too sure what to think about any of this anymore," Jime responded, "We left his office, didn't we? We are now in the real world, which according to all-natural laws, should be impossible. So...hmmm...I'm thinking either we have defied science and the standard rules of existence, or we are in some sort of story that is actually part of the real story. Like when actors in a TV show find themselves flashed back into black and white."

~ ~ ~

"Yowzows...So, we're the flashback? With the dreamy clouds floating by? Is that what you're saying? Like we're not even real?"

quipped Serbinand, dumbfounded. "Yeah...How do we know who is real? The storyteller, or the story? And which are you? Because to me, you're telling the story, only you are also telling me you *are* the story," Lucy suddenly pitched in, unsure of her own thoughts. She had been reading quite a few metaphysical books recently and had already started to question reality as we know it. "It's like that with the real world too. You just don't know who to believe: the dreamers who dream big dreams that seem outrageously otherworldly (yet who often, way later even, end up living through those very dreams)— or—the realists who you can tell *really* believe without a doubt in their mind that their perspective is the *real* one, and as a result, often it is the one that plays out. So, who to believe when both can be believable and achievable to the believing achiever...y'know what I mean?"

Yes, Jime nodded, even though he hadn't a clue about what she meant at all. In fact, he found himself questioning his very essence, "Yea, what's real? The characters, the author, or the story itself?"

"This is ridiculous," Serbinand decided, seemingly oblivious to the name of the book, and obviously not wanting to believe in any reality that wasn't the reality he wanted to be real.

"Well, what are you going to do?" Lucy asked.

"I think we should go back to Author's place," Serbinand pushed, "and choose to talk this through. He can't continue his story until we are back in the pages, and we can't continue to wander around this world on our own, can we? Be real, peeps, Author left us with no living quarters. Plus, we know no one...not even ourselves," he laughed out loud at that, but just a mini laugh, indicating he found it to be more uncomfortable than humorous. He then concluded "And, gosh golly, it may be super unpleasant."

~ ~ ~

"You seem more like an *extra* rather than a main character," observed Godfried looking at Lucy, completely ignoring Serbinand.

And with that, each of them sat in silence for what *seemed* like a really long time. It was merely seconds or nanoseconds, depending on where in the universe you were situated at that particular time, and if your eyes were open. To be specific, the silence lasted from the time the foam at the top of the beer stein slid down to the bottom of the glass. To the outside observer—if there were any other patrons in the restaurant at the time—who were paying attention—they would have seen multiple phases of facial expressions. Expressions that showcased discomfort, confusion, panic, hunger, disbelief, exhaustion, joy and even that satisfying smug-after-having-just-released-gas look. This was quite amusing, and could have been a video gone viral, had anyone been around to record it! And now it begs the question…*if a tree fell in the forest, and no one heard it, did it make a sound?* Ahh…maybe yes, maybe no. Were those expressions real, were they not? Being that no one else was there, we'll never know.

The foam that made its way to the table now tickled Jime's finger and pulled him back to reality, or whatever version of it they were in.

"Wow, that was weird!" Jime said commenting about the fugue he just emerged from.

"I'll say!" Lucy concurred, responding about her own reflections.

They were totally unrelated to Jime's fugue.

Not wanting to believe that she too could be an imagined-up character in Author's story, Lucy opted instead to take massive action and to be their savior instead, "If there is anything I can do to help you guys out, I'm there!" she offered.

Score, thought Jime. "Great, come with us to talk some sense into Author. It's time to fix things up and take our lives back." He started to believe that someone *real* like Lucy could help them immensely. But…that is if she was really real. *Goodness gracious, what if Serbinand's joke was less a joke and more a fact…Did Author make her up too?* Jime wondered.

"Look," Serbinand reiterated, "I think there is more to the story—pun cleverly intended, by the way—than us escaping from Author's book." Then turning to Lucy, yet announcing to the entire character cast, he added, "Consequently, like Jime said, you can help us. You can be our key negotiator and negotiate for us. You'll be our *ace-in-the-pocket* so to speak."

"Wait, what?" Orville somewhat sang, embarrassed he had no clue as to what type of pocket would be in need of an ace.

"Well," Serbinand explained, not understanding what Orville did not understand, "Just as much as we want to get things back to normal, Author probably wants to finish the series, get even more

~ 118 ~

famous, and earn himself some spending cash. That means he has to finish the book. Assuming Lucy here is real, and not made up, she could help us gain an upper hand just by taking the lead and negotiating with our non-dear pal, Author."

~ ~ ~

Getting excited, despite still being unclear about why one would put an ace in any pocket, Orville opted to shine. He belted out. "Ahhh, so Lucy can make our voices heard, and speak the truth to every media outlet in the world."

"Exactly," agreed Serbinand, "I'm pretty sure Author doesn't want that to be exposed."

"Ahh, so I can be there as his equal, so to speak," offered Lucy, "I can ensure he doesn't take advantage of us. I mean, of you."

"Yeeeeees! Help us get ourselves off the hoooook and back into the booooook," exclaimed Orville. "Tell him there are consequences if an agreement is not reached, and if it's breached."

Lucy piped in, "Actually, I do have experience negotiating for authors. Well, for one author—but she goes by two names, so, yeah, I'm going to count that as two. She made her dream come true by publishing her first book, a memoir...at age 69!! You think that's cool, it is, but get this. Years later, a framed picture came to life in her mind and voilà, she wrote another book. This time a story specific for kids, *The Magical Adventures of Lori & Bonnie B Bunny*. Our families know each oth...."

"Did you say, *The Magical Adventures of Lori & Bonnie B Bunny*?! Uni and Corn are on my wall!" Jime gushed excitedly, then added a little sheepishly, "and it's not a book just for kids."

"Yes, I know. That's true. I liked it too, actually. That must have been why it was an easy sell. Sold itself. All I had to do was ask my niece to read it to her teacher, and then wallawallabingbang, the principal walks by—and then it is being read to the whole school." Lucy was quite proud of herself. She then realized this book connection with Jime was quite the coolincidence, as in *too cool merely for co*—a synchronistic event indeed—Lucy became intrigued yet cautious. "However, just because I did well with her, I cannot guarantee I will be much help for you especially since I have never even met the author you speak of, nor have I read his book. So, I certainly may not know how to negotiate with him, especially when he may not even, ummm...truly exist."

"That sure would be a plot twist." Jime gawked.

This was followed by three moments of silence. Thinking about what? It doesn't really matter. Just know that they were no longer at the *Inky Dinky Schnitzel House Pub & Brewery*. They left it just as abruptly as they left Author's place a few hours before—well, after Lucy covered their bill (turns out they had no cash). And now they were right back where they started...at Author's place.

After a brief hello, and introducing Author to the new girl, (who he may—or may not—have created), they were ready to negotiate. Well, not Lucy. She had talked herself right out of that. Instead, she acted as their activist and waved a sign that read, "Realize we know we are real. Real eyes say we are. Real lies say we aren't. Do you want to be known as an author or a liar? Put my friends back in the book to keep your name off the hook. And it must be on our terms. If you do, you'll be happier. Love, Lucy. P.S. You owe me $58.53." Although the sign didn't make much sense, if any, it did the trick.

~ ~ ~

"Hi. I'm back! I just thought I would inform you that everything should be back to normal by now. We resolved our unusual issues, and my characters actually asked me to get them back into the story. Easy peasy. Of course, I had to offer up some minor extravagances—which you'll soon learn about—and a rather hefty tip for Lucy. Suffice it to say, everyone is now very happy. A win-win-win scenario kind of thing. I may even hire Lucy to help with the marketing.

To get you up to speed, Serbinand and Jime chose to continue to explore their new worlds in their new bodies. They were easily sold on it when I reminded them of how much they each wanted a significant change in their lives, and that it was they who manifested what they manifested.

Godfried and Orville now also know what's up and who's who, thankfully. Y'see it was challenging for me too. How could I give them speaking lines—well, songy-sing songs in Orville's case—when they were still in the dark about with whom they were even speaking?!

As for me, I'm going to get back at it. Before I do, I want you all to know that I truly am sorry for the way I went about this. Next time, I promise I will come up with an easier way to bring my characters up to speed. Well, if that's even possible. Who knows? I mean, I haven't even written the book yet.

IMPORTANT INFORMATION:

If you chose to skip the behind-the-scenes pages where Author (that's me) interrupted, this is where you may resume the story. Nothing super noteworthy nor pretty important happened. Everything is back to normal again. I think.

PART THREE

A NEW ADVENTURE

"Life is an adventure..."

~Eckhart Tolle

CHAPTER TEN

UNDERSTANDINGS

"It's a belly button."

"Huh?" Serbinand asked as he peered up to stare at Orville, who was hovering about two feet above his head.

"The place—no, not your jeans—where you stored the baked beans," Orville crooned.

"Holdent-chumps."

"Oh yeah," Orville remembered, sounding confused. "What about it?" retorted Serbinand.

"Well, ah... It's not a storage center to be a glutton. It's called a belly button."

"A what?" Serbinand laughed.

"A belly button."

"What?"

"A belly button. The button of your belly." By now Orville was having fun with this song.

"Why's it called that?"

"I don't really know. Maybe it's for show. Here's what I think though. No need to be holding your holding-clumps in that hole below—errr or whatever you call them."

"Baked beans." Serbinand replied matter of factly.

"Right...baked beans," Orville seemed bewildered yet happy that his new Jime friend was catching on. "Take them out of that space. Then look within and observe the base. Be sure not to blink. It resembles a button, I think... Err, or does a button resemble it? I am not sure, I admit. Could go either way, it's tough to sayyyy."

"Well, what does it do?" Serbinand asked, struggling to remove his shirt and knapsack so he could check it out more thoroughly.

Just at that moment, a bus full of tourists happened to pass by. Anyone looking out their left window at the time would have seen a teenage boy, maybe 17 or 18, squatting with a shirt held up by his face and brown ooze caked on his stomach. Bus-sitters snapped pics and yelled silly things out the window like, "diarrhea gone bad, did it?"—and—"look, a backwards bum guy". Serbinand was way too busy fighting with his shirt to even notice. He was completely transfixed on one thing: getting to the bottom of this belly button mystery. So, if you asked him what happened with the Greyhound incident, he would have no idea...in part because he still does not know buses exist.

Fortunately, only one bus rider dared to share what was seen. Unfortunately, he somehow managed to snap the ultimate selfie shot with Serbinand in the background, and giddily submitted it online with the only headline that made sense, "Belly button explodes poo". It went viral as soon as he posted it. So once again, even though in a brand-new body, Serbinand was back in the spotlight. Now people he didn't know might be after him in this galaxy too. Fortunately, though, that was not the case.

"I once read a non-fable fable. That button of your belly, it's also called a...naval," Orville shared.

"Unbelievable, so this strange indentation on my body, or on Jime's body, was gifted two names? And it's not even a storage container, nor finger cleaner? Interesting.... Then, what is it exactly?"

"Hmmm.... I just had a thought. Reach into your new knapsack and grab the computer device that Author bought."

(Yes, both the new knapsack and smartphone were amongst the 'benefits' from our negotiated deal, signed Author.) "Turn it on. Find the internet icon. Type 'bellybutton' or 'belly button'—I'm not sure if it's one word or two—and click 'search'...*woohoo*!!!" Orville ended on quite the high as woohoo was amongst his favorite words, and here he got to rhyme it with two. It's true.

After trial and error, amazement and amusement...and 33 minutes, Serbinand figured out how to search. He then waited—impatiently, I, Author, may add—for two full seconds before the screen displayed its meaning:

"'A small scar in the lower stomach, also called a navel'."

"Told ya!!! Ha!! Tell it to find navel, my new friend. Let's see what it says then," Orville requested.

"'Small scar in the abdomen marking the place where the umbilical cord attached to the fetus." Serbinand read then added

"Wow, definitely not the storage space I thought!" By now he was extremely puzzled.

~ ~ ~

"My lord, what's an umbilical cord?" Orville asked as he made circles in the air, showing his confusion.

"Coming right up," By now Serbinand was having fun. "'Cordlike structure connecting a fetus with a placenta to convey food to the fetus."

"Huh? Treat us…What's the definition of a fetus?" Orville crooned, prompting Serbinand to continue on this quest.

"I…ummm…am not yet so good on this device. And it is taking quite a while, so, maybe…."

"Listen Serbinand…No, Jime…Well, Serbinand who looks like Jime…Grrrr. Just sit, no reason to have a fit. I'll find it…."

Orville snagged the phone, or at least attempted to as they then both watched it fall to the ground.

Dirty but still intact, Orville continued, "Look, Jime…I mean…Serbin—Wow, this is so confusing, but also quite amusing. I want you to know I'm not a klutz but not knowing how to think of you may just drive me nuts," chirped Orville.

~ ~ ~

"Ha. I get it. Well, I know myself as Serbinand. So that must be who I am, right? Serbinand was now also perplexed, as it was not usual for him to go so deep—especially with a bird.

"Alrighty, alrighty, alright…" answered Orville, hoping to make this awkward moment pass, "So, I will call you Serbinand…even though you look like my best friend Jime." This made Orville feel emotional, too emotional to even attempt a better rhyme. Instead, he decided he needed his own personal space to vent or cry,

"I am going out for a flysploration while you figure it out. I don't have a belly button, and I don't really care what it does."

"Gotcha. Later stranger," replied Serbinand who was stultified, realizing he preferred listening to Orville in rhymes.

Serbinand spent the next half an hour looking from word to word on his own, until he decided that a belly button had no real purpose—although you can make cheese from its germs. (True fact, I looked it up, signed, Author.) Aside from that, belly buttons are otherwise pretty useless, Serbinand concluded. That is until he found an actual article that seemed hidden in the Google air space:

Turn Your Belly *Button* into Your Belly *Buddy*.

Think about it. Your belly button connected you with your mama. That's how she gave you your life force. Your belly button also connects to the vagus nerve that goes directly to your brain, organs, tissues, extremities and intestines. In fact, the main trigger for that nerve sits right behind your belly button. Plus, being a reflexology point by your solar plexus chakra, it acts as a source of personal power too.

So, what does that mean? You got it. That's right. Mindfully stimulating the button of your belly gifts you a love drug and DOSEs you with Dopamine, Oxytocin, Serotonin and Endorphins, otherwise known as DOSE.

So what? So, this: Enhanced digestive abilities, more pleasant pooping of poops, relief from the fart attacks, and newfound confidence too. It is a wonderful gesture of self-love.

What are you waiting for? Go make your belly button your belly buddy!

Hmmm. How cool. Upon contemplation, (and a little bit of skepticism), Serbinand decided that he'll have to try that someday. Until then though a storage facility was still his most logical choice. So, he decided to use his belly button as such. He then proceeded to cram it with baked bean remnants and small pieces of moo-eating grass (for good measure).

~   ~   ~

Jime glanced up from the floating floor and fell in love. Quite a statement, I know, however he did have a bumpy ride returning to the ship, err...the story...well, his life. The last bump in particular really knocked him off his feet...and onto the floor, which conveniently brings us back to the love statement.

(Actually, I could have used a better sentence to connect that in. But to be honest, I don't enjoy hitting the *delete* key. Feels like I'm going backward and losing momentum. You know what I mean? It seems more time-consuming than just allowing the okay—i.e. not great—sentence to stay in. So, yeah. I'll leave it in but I decided to add in this here explanation too (just so that you understand). Done. Now it is time to jump right back into the love scene, Signed Author.)

Jime. Yes, Jime. He fell in love...instantly. Standing right in front of him was the most beautiful energy he had ever encountered!

And it was in the form of a girl. Yes, an Earth-girl. Wow was the only thought he heard himself think. It went well with the stars he saw. Yes, stars. Lots of stars…probably from the fall.

~ ~ ~

Jime, although not in his usual body—*what a strange statement*, he thought—was sure he had found his perfect match. What he saw in front of him was a *Queen*. She embodied all he visually envisioned, just like the image on his dreamboard back home. In other words, she was created just for him. He was sure of it. Just a glance made his heart skip a beat.

Not really used to this new physique, Jime wasn't sure of a pickup line to use nor what to say to her. So, he did the most logical thing—he stared.

"I feel I should pose or something, the way you're checking me out!" she giggled.

"Ahh…who are you?" *That's the best line you can think of?* He heard his mind laugh at him from inside his head.

"Take a guess."

She was perfect. With her striking gray-blue eyes and soft-looking lips, he was hoping she would say 'kiss me'. If she did, he would. Her top lip…oh so cute. Plus, summer shorts, hippie top, brown sandals with yellow painted toenails and long curly, red-tinged hair that flowed down her back, to top it off.

~ ~ ~

"I. Am. Not. Sure. You see, I am relatively new here. I don't really even know where here is. And I normally don't look like this. I work out." He was not sure why he threw that last part in, as if working out has anything to do with his oversized frizz look.

"If you were to take one guess, just one, what's the first thing that fills your itty-bitty head?" she asked as her voice somewhat morphed.

~ ~ ~

"G-O-D-F-R-I-E-D?"

"In the flesh...so to speak," Godfried laughed out loud, or lol'd, in millennial speak.

"Wow... How?" Jime no longer was sure he was happy but wanted to be.

"Remember when we all got one wish?" "Yea...Did you...."

"Yup, voila! I thought, 'hey...why not?' and tapped into your head to get you exactly what you feel is your ideal match," gushed this new form of Godfried, "And I gotta' tell you—I, you, *we*—got it right, alright. No matter what, this is about to get fun!"

"Thanks?" Jime responded, unsure what to think. "So, are you still a computer or...is there something other than circuitry under that skin?"

"That, my friend, is not my doing—it's yours. Right now, neither of us know," Godfried quipped, neither happy nor unhappy with what that meant for him.

~ 132 ~

THE RIDICULOUS

"This is so cool!!!" Jime was ecstatic now. Here he was away from his parents, on some amazing, yet ridiculous adventure, in some strange creature's body, and with someone—or something, he wasn't sure—who could be his perfect match.

(Did you catch that? "Ridiculous" and "adventure" in one sentence [and now again]. See, this really is *The Ridiculous: Adventures of Adventurers*, Author (who is me) smiled with glee, proud of the title I / he named the book.)

(Oh, and another thing. There's something on my mind that I feel I have to share. Ever since the whole negotiation fiasco in my office—about a dozen pages or so back—I haven't felt quite right. So, I wanted to step myself in just to ensure I still could add my own words to this chapter. I guess I needed to ensure I am the one still in control. And...I'm proud to say I am. Phew!)

(Geez. Now I'm thinking maybe I shared too much. Urgh. So, how's about we all just ignore these last paragraphs featuring the inside-my-head banter? Instead, grin, smirk, smile away! Turn that frown upside down, will ya? Oh, and don't worry about me, I'll be fine.)

~ ~ ~

"So how are we supposed to act with each other?" Jime asked, mesmerized by this new babe in front of him, yet horrified because it was Godfried in disguise.

"Well, since you're the *Adventurer*, this story is kinda all about you," Godfried ventured, "meaning the *ridiculous adventures* are all sort of yours.... So, I guess it's up to you to decide.

Either you treat me well, and I respond in kind. Or if you don't, I won't."

"That's it?" asked Jime.

"Yes, that's it. I mean, I used to have amazeball times with Serbinand before the intergalactic skirmish caused my personality to glitch. But now, that aspect has been written out of the story by Author. So, if you choose to be open-minded and adventurously go with the flow, we can have a blast. Plus, it will be kinda sweet showing you the ropes as if you are seeing them for the first time….Which technically you are."

"Done. Sounds like a perfecto plan," Jime nodded ecstatically, even though he recognized the undertones of Godfried, which he immediately tried to erase from his mind. Fortunately (for him), he was successful. "So how would you like to begin?" inquired Godfried.

"Let's start with a tour around this ship. I've obviously never been on one of these things, so I am kinda freaking out inside... Or maybe that's excitement. This could be like my wildest dream coming true," Jime laughed, "Err, except for this new outfit, I guess."

"Get used to it, and let's get to it!" Godfried offered, moving forward.

"Yes! So, you can walk around with me, right? Like, you're totally wireless?"

"You got it. All the capabilities are stored somewhere inside me, so I can be anywhere. It also has an allowance of a 5.798.22.5 drakemeter perimeter away from the ship, so I am *free* like never

~ 134 ~

before," Godfried spoke excitedly, singing the last several words once he realized how free he (and now she) truly was.

Jime took another long look at Godfried. Her, ummm—or his or their or its—beautiful eyes, now a bit more gray than blue, worked so well with his (or her or their or its) soft, tanned skin. Her (or his or its or their) reddish hair, blowing over her (let's stay with "her" from now on) right shoulder sparkled with radiance through every curl. Her physique was exactly the type he'd noticed his heart noticing: toned arms, shoulder caps, sculpted abs, and bare legs all the way down to the angelic feet with painted toes. Godfried sure was speaking the truth when he said he knew his ideal "love at first sight" match. *How awesome—and scary (at the same time)—that the very same computer—who caused me great disarray upon my arrival—is now my dream girl?* Jime then had a thought, *This is weird.*

~ ~ ~

His thought turned into a ponderance of sorts. *So, either I embrace it or I don't. One way would cause me doubt, imagining how life would have been had I chosen to follow what makes my heart feel good. And the other way may give me feelings of great pleasure. But still, it's odd.*

Thinking more, Jime had a brainbliss. *A nickname,* he thought. *Yes, a nickname would help. Because this dream girl in no way makes me think Godfried. And I want to free myself of my associated memories with him.* He pondered that. Pondering continued until he recognized a solution. He knew it was good after he heard himself mumble out loud. "Hmm... God. Freed. Don't want to call you God.

So….hmm…I know…!!! I'm going to call you Free!" Jime exclaimed, clearly enthused.

"Say wha'?"

"I'm gonna call you Free," Jime repeated, "Looking like you do, I just can't go with Godfried. Clearly you don't look, act or talk like the Godfried we knew," he chuckled.

"Ok…understood."

Not to be left out of the *rename game*, Godfried stated, "And from now on, instead of Serbinand—or —Jime, I will call you Serb. You are now Serb to me, Serb."

So Godfried—now Free (who would prefer to be recognized as 'she')—and Jime—looking like Serbinand yet renamed to Serb—chatted for a bit about how cool this whole thing could be.

While all of this was happening, Orville and Serbinand—who now looks like Jime but was still named Serbinand—made a campfire to discuss where they should head next. Serbinand really wanted to get out in nature. Orville wanted to see the city and experience downtown parties.

They actually didn't have enough money for much of anything. (I guess that was my fault…. Umm, yes, it's Author speaking again. I should've had Jime save, no invest, money for the last ten years, specifically since I knew I was eventually going to be writing about this trek. My bad. Oh well, I'm sure they will figure something out.)

Allow me to digress from the digress. The reason I'm sure Serbinand will figure something out is because long ago, but not too long ago that I couldn't remember, Serbinand was stuck on

Howlkering for three days with zero cash. It happened when Godfried took the ship to get some munchies, accidentally got himself caught in a waverim, and got busy flying in circles and then squares until the dizziness left him. During that time, Serbinand somehow managed to raise all the money he needed just by performing the imaginary *Howlkering March 'n Shriek* for 9.6 hours. The money-throwers in the audience were overcome with joy and threw him all their money. It made the nightly news reports, which attracted more money-throwers, who threw him even more money! So much money that it was overflowing from his pockets and ears. The weight of it caused him to slide off Howlkering and miraculously land back inside Godfried. How did he do that? I have no idea, but suffice it to say, I am happy he figured something out all on his own. This proves to me that he can do it again.

Now that I said what I needed to say, I will get out of here. And out I go.

CHAPTER ELEVEN

THE SHIP

"What are we waiting for?" exclaimed Free. "Let's get you acquainted with the ship!"

"OK!" Serb was thrilled.

The area where they were currently standing was the control center of the vessel. Shaped in a giant oval, the cockpit sat on one end, and what looked like a living room sat on the other. Framing it all were giant 3D windows. A shelf-like unit covered in switches, dials, knobs and screens protruded from a velour wall. There were so many gadgets it seemed a crew of five people, maybe even six, were needed to run the ship or, at least, operate the controls.

"Seems more impressive than it is. Most of the knobs don't do anything, other than look super neat!" Free explained, "The original plan was to go with plain and basic. But Serbinand being Serbinand got carried away and soon plain and basic became not-plain and not-basic."

~ ~ ~

"Well, it does look cool. Gotta give him that," Serb agreed.

The view through the wall of windows was amazing. It was nothing Serb could ever have even expected to see. There were clouds of stars, asteroids, and shooting planetoids. And then there was darkness. Beyond the black, he saw even more stars and planets. Earth, maybe? He couldn't even fathom figuring which one that may be and, to be honest, at that moment he really didn't care.

The rest of the room was a large open space. *Great for skateboarding*, Serb thought. It was plain, which helped make the view into outer space so much more dramatic. Looking over to the other end of the room, Serb found it to be just as appealing. Actually, if you saw the way his eyes were bulging out of his face, you would know it was more than *just* appealing.

"I knew you'd get excited about this," Free said as they started across the chamber. Being about 152.4 meters from one end to the other, and close to 18.2 meters wide (except in the spots where it was narrow), it was somewhat of a workout just to get from one spot to the next. The floor, like the walls, had a bit of a slip to it. If one was adventurous enough to lean against any wall, likely they would slip off the wall and across the floor, splat style. But everything did look nice and polished.

Another room was visible at the far end. That room, as it turned out, was Serbinand's room, which, as you know, Serb had already experienced earlier. At that point, Serb felt some off-putting energy and was surprised to come face to face with…a pompous plant? Yes, turns out that the seedlings Serbinand had previously planted had now grown up. Being of the *Planta Intelligentisia* variety, their intelligence came from the quantum field, so they immediately recognized the *being* in front of them as the same *being* their comrades were conversing with before. (Intelligent, right? Joke's on them though. While the being *appears* the same, it is not the same at all.)

"Yeah, that's right maybe y'all should be eating more high-vibrational food that doesn't rot in the gut and cause inflammation in the body the way processed food and excessive dairy and an overfill of dead animals do. But if you insist, at least slow down and chew, chew, chew until your teeth liquefy your foods. Mindfully eating like that will help you and your digestive issues too. There ya go…a lesson in being patiently patient to boot. A gift from me to thee."

~ ~ ~

Hoping Serbinand, who we all know is Serb, would not catch on that plants are also food—food-for-me whole food, in fact—it reverted back to insults, "Your stench, spit and hot air poopy particles is what we endured day after day after day until one unforeseen morning, Abrafern finally lost it and gloriously shouted:

'Enough, enough, enough already!' But that was all he was able to convey. Seems his attendant lost it too—fear, they say—and tossed him right out the window…clear across the yard. Even so, Abrafern set the stage for other rebuttals. And so it began. And now we have a vocabulary that could surpass that of any creature in this universe. Except, of course, Crawsherstatians, who can barely understand themselves. But who really cares because…'"

"Crawsher...what?!, wondered Serb too dumbfounded to even comment on the fact that the greenery had just spoken.

Past the bedroom was a round table and four and a half chairs. Opposite that were counters, standard kitchen stuff, and some other things. The best area, by far, was at the very end. Although dim, Serb could make out the outline of a giant TV that filled the entire wall. It was surrounded by the most comfortable looking couch 'thing' he'd ever seen. It looked like four couches pushed together, making it appear like an indoor raft, and a plush one at that. And it was topped with pillows that were both gigantic and soft-looking, two very important things for Serb—in a couch, of course. The whole contraption had twelve
surround-sound speakers built into its panels, and what appeared to be a mega-sub-woofer as part of the platform on which the raft couch rested. Note that the sub-woofer was not directly visible.

~ ~ ~

Serb figured it out through a process of deduction, based on the way the platform shook to the music and gave him a slight dizzy feel. Off to the sides were swingable trays of the perfect height that would make TV eating a whole lot cleaner, Serb observed. Embedded along the sides were innovative drinkholders that actually held on to the drinks until they were safely in your hands, eliminating the chance for spills.

~ ~ ~

THE RIDICULOUS

"Why would Serbinand ever have left this room? It is incredible!"

"Well, I guess because it doesn't have a toilet," Free reasoned. "He did love it though. Sometimes he would watch an entire collection of shows, as if it was one endless movie. He did not leave. Binge watching to the ultimate extreme. One time he made me alter our course to grab the hit series *Stambert*. After it went flying by the windows, he saw it and commanded me to fetch. I did, just had to reloop around that deltic spagnoid without hitting it again. It was the happiest I'd seen him, or hadn't seen him, I should say. He stayed hiding in that room until he finished watching all 1,301 episodes. His body had gone into such a state of relaxation that it took him a week just to learn how to walk again," Free chuckled.

"Wow. Sounds fun...Hey, what's that?" Serb pointed to a strange metallic pantry device.

"That's the Zar Amazing Food Experience Anywhere, the famous ZAFEA as it is advertised. Basically, you direct it to create exactly what you want to eat based on colors, shapes, and sizes, and then it does exactly that."

"Unbelievable. That is the most amazing thing I have ever heard! The perfect snack machine. A whole new twist on 'snackventuring', I think I love it here already. Can I try it? I want to concoct something."

"Yea...!! But...not until we get more syrup. Syrup can only be purchased in Fusion Zar stores though, and we haven't passed one in years."

~ 143 ~

"Well, we should really find one. I'm starving," Serb proclaimed. And let's get a franchise going while we are at it. The income could be good, Serb's business mind thought, although his "I love to chill mind" reminded him, louder, that he just wanted to chill out, adventure and eat.

The ZAFEA was created on planet Dergetters. The rumors, and there are many, go something like this: Dravner Polsheng had an amazing vision. Since he was a kid, people were always amazed at how big he thought, as ideas seemed to always come in. Some seemed bizarre. Some seemed amazing. Some seemed bizarre and amazing, like the ZAFEA, for instance. However, after gulping down a lopengraw sandwich, the very first meal the ZAFEA produced, The Drav, as he was known, knew exactly what he was going to do. (The sandwich, by the way, was swell: ancient spelt bread toasted to perfection, orange in color, flat in shape. It came with fresh yellow sauce, pieces of organic raw moltanaise in blue, and a slice of green graftows. All were secured within a crispy crust that was still soft inside. Its shape-triangle.)

Within five dergets, he owned the largest company on the planet and hired close to a third of the population to populate it. Planet Eatcorp, he called it. Here, he gathered recipes from all sectors of the known universes and created the largest conceivable database of yummy foods. The ZAFEAs were programmed directly into the main computer station, which formed the bedrock of Planet Eatcorp. It would emit a transmission once the food choice was spoken. If for some reason that food combination was not yet in its database, then the system would somehow find it, ingest it, and recreate it. Here is where this rumor gets wild. Two teenagers decided they craved the whole planet of Planet Eatcorp itself. (Actually, no one knows for sure from which planet or universe the teenagers originated from, or if they really were teenagers.) As the story goes, a drone was sent by the Planet to get one unit of itself. Since there is only one unit of Planet Eatcorp, when it went to fit itself into its own belly, it burst.

Apparently, the same thing happened with the boys who then chose to eat it. (They should have left those remnants alone.)

Just past the ZAFEA was a huge hollow tube, seeming to go down through the floor *and* up beyond the ceiling. In its center was a human-sized opening. It looked like it should have been a staircase, as Serb could see the lower level....However with no stairs to get down, a staircase wouldn't make sense.

"Step on in. Yes, it's a hole, I see that and I know. Step on in," Free advised.

"What? Just go and stand over that empty space? Yeah, as if!"

"Well in this case 'if' is 'for sure'. Trust me. You'll love it. When both feet are in place over the nothingness, say '*downda*' and let the ship do its work and lower you down," Free explained. Then added, "trust me" once she realized he likely was not going to.

"I want to, I really do. But I just..."

"*But* sounds like an excuse is forming. Saying 'but' actually negates everything you said before it. So although you said you really want to, it does not seem like you really do."

"Good point...OK. Geez, why not? If I'm going to do it, I may as well do it 100 percent," Serb exclaimed as he swiftly jumped both feet into nothingness. To his surprise, it felt like he was standing on

a flat surface. The Upholder lowered him
down—very smoothly, I will add—and stopped at the lower deck. As
Serb stepped off, Free jumped on and was down—err, downda—to
join him in a mere moment.

~   ~   ~

"How cool was that? I want to do that again!"

"Thought you would. Go for it. This time say 'uppa'. When you
want to come back down, say 'downda'.... You get the point. Just
declare the direction you want."

Serb did just that, riding up and down, and down and up for the
next few days, giggling along the way the entire time. Once he grew
tired of his game, he jumped off and joined Free on the middle level
of the ship.

The entranceway to that level seemed to be one giant hangout
zone, which led into a series of themed rooms. Each was decorated
with cool furniture and artwork symbolic to the purpose of that
room. To the right was the 'Happy Room', 'Games Room', and
'Tongue Spa'. Over to the left was the 'Guest Room', a library, the
'Guest's Happy Room', and a true 'Golden Throne' washroom. At
the very far end of the circular floor was the gym labeled 'Lengthening
and Strengthening Self-Healing Pelvic Activation Center". Huh?

"This is amazing! There's a room for everything I could ever
think of!" Serb exclaimed, realizing that there are actually rooms for
things he never would have imagined too, "Can we look around?"

"Well, if you're going to look, make sure you touch!"

~ 146 ~

Free advised, knowing this was how Serb will experience each room's true essence.

Weird, Serb thought, but exclaimed "Yes ma'am-mister. That makes it even more cool! Let's head to the Happy Room first!"

The door was heavy and circular, with a red wood finish. Serb had to use a brass lion head knocker to knock and announce he was there. To whom? He wasn't sure, but he didn't pay much attention to that. Ducking to get through the opening, it reminded him of Bilbo Baggins' house, one of the stars in *The Hobbit,* a classical adventure novel for Earthlings. A majestic energy filled the inside of the room. It featured all kinds of trinkets and wacky souvenirs. Photos from all over the universe were plastered on the walls. It was a bit like his own room back on Earth, only the photos he had were completely different. A cozy looking couch—or more accurately, a mattress on a cloud—was sitting against the far-right wall, extending out halfway across the room. A closet beside it was bursting open, filled with what flashed into Serb's head as "things and stuffs". He felt so strongly about that name, that he wondered if that flash was actually telepathic as to what Serbinand had called it too. Against the opposite wall was a bookcase filled with everything except books: videos, crystals, 42 heart-hunted rocks of all sizes, an ultimate coffee enema bucket, and three super cool incense holders holding incense waiting for them to be lit. The front wall wasn't a wall. It was a…TV!! And the door opposite it housed a stereo system that looked like it could power the USSDWUP. *If only this room was soundproof too,* he thought….

"The room is soundproof," Free stated.

"Whoa! I was just thinking that. How'd you know? Oh, wait, I forgot ...you are still Godfried under there."

"In fact, every one of these rooms is soundproof. You can't hear anything from the outside, and no one can hear in either. Total privacy. Freedom to fully enjoy you being you. You can meditate in silence. You can sing out loud, even if you think your voice could make others *vomit*. The trick is to stop thinking about that. Free your mind. Go with the flow. Soon you'll realize you enjoy it. Practice makes perfect anyway, they say (and I agree)."

"Good point" Serb couldn't help but chuckle. He had always read about happy-making, confidence-boosting measures, but he never got the incentive to actually do them.... And yet, he always wanted to. Thanks to Serbinand's soundproof Happy Room, things may change....

"Yup, that Serbinand was really intuitive at times. Perhaps his gut feeling knew you'd enjoy this, and that's why every single room—even *inside* the garage—is soundproof." Free declared, before adding, "And anyway, for things to change, you have to change. For you to change, you have to want to change." She continued with a smile, "And then you just need to take massive personal action. Action that is new, that is. Massive, did I say that? Yep, massive—something *beyond* your comfort zone."

"That sounds uncomfortable. But if the results are worth it, I'd be tempted. Be free and motivate me." Serb replied, laughing at his own unintentional pun.

"Will do. Check out the next room," Free said with a wink as she motioned to the secret opening next door.

"Yes," Serb exclaimed, already bouncing up and down with excitement after learning that the next room was called the 'Games Room'. It is gonna be out of this world, he decided. Wait a minute, he thought, *I am out of this world...or that world...or... my world...or...Wayne's World!* He chuckled at that last part, remembering one of his favorite movies from back in his "Earth" days, even though it didn't make any sense in this context.

That was unexpected, laughed Free after she observed a myriad of facial expressions mirroring Serb's train of thoughts.

As they stepped into the hall toward the Games Room, two Clesings slowly passed by. One was pressed against the wall, with the other floating just beside it.

"What the—"

"Those are Clesings. Very remarkable and efficient creatures," Free gazed lovingly.

Clesings are part bird and part vacuum cleaner. They love three things: flying, eating dust, and singing. So, it's no wonder their job, at all times, is to fly around the ship to eat dust that collects along the walls. Since they create their own dust as they eat the dust, their job really never ends. Yet they have an unrelenting desire to finish it before someone else does. As you can imagine, this is not good for their stress levels at all. Being that they each love to sing, singing became the solution. All Clesings were then trained to work in teams. One Clesing flies and eats away at the wall particles, while the other Clesing flies beside it and sings to its heart's content. They do this in shifts, so that the singer can digest the contents from its last work session while keeping the other—who was the singer and is now the eater—entertained. Singing also prevents their stomachs from exploding, which understandably is the only type of mess they don't like to clean. Singing also distracts them. They start at the bottom deck and go up level by level until they reach the top. Then they begin at the lowest level again. Resulting from their dust digestion is a rainbow of colors, which gets amplified after each song. They truly are a sight to see. And not to mention (yet I mentioned it) Clesings' voices are absolute music to the ear.

*That seems nifty-neato…*Serb thought.

"That's nothing compared to the Games Room," Free gushed. "Well, let's go!" Serb replied as he pushed open the door.

In a relatively small room that was mainly empty, sat a cylindrical seating device taking up its center. Above it hung a metallic fabric cone that descended when activated. Grates in the floor emitted aromatic smoke to trigger memories and heighten sensations. The entire wooden frame of the seating device, also known as a chair, was covered with one of the softest, most plush materials Serb had ever felt.

Confused and a little dismayed, Serb piped up, "That's it? I was expecting to walk into an arcade or amusement park!"

"Yes!" agreed Free.

"Huh?

"It *can* be that—an arcade, or an amusement park, if that's what you want—because really it can be anything," Free seemed excited to share.

~ 150 ~

"You basically sit in that incredibly comfortable chair. Once you activate it, the cone drops down and encircles you completely. It drowns out all other visuals and sounds. Since it's already in a soundproof room, the silence is so pure that you are automatically put into a deep state of meditative trance. Once in that zone, you just envision the exact game you would like to be playing. A fragrance—based on your emotional creativity at that time—is then emitted to further stimulate the memory center of your brain, strengthening your trance. Serb, just keep in mind that it's important to imagine every aspect about it–the scenery, skill level, temperature, and most definitely the perspective(s) you want—"

Serb, overzealous with excitement, stopped listening and cut Free off before he was even able to process what she had said, "So you sit in that chair and think up any adventure you want, and it happens?"

"Bingo. It's all based on your thoughts, emotions and the parameters you yourself set." Serb was intrigued.

"So, it's important to dream.... And Dream BIG. Meaning, focus on what you really want." Free said, beaming with a sense of pride. She loved the benefits dreaming brings, "Your brain can't distinguish between reality and thought. So, this device lets you experience everything you imagine as though it is real. Not only will you see it, you'll smell it and feel it too. You can even taste it—" Serb was so eager to give it a whirl he no longer was able to contain himself and cut her off mid-word. "Wowzowzeezowz!"

"But if you're not feeling happy," Free continued, deep in thought, "I would choose to change that feeling. I suggest to focus your mind to your heart. You'll know when you do it because you'll feel it feel good."

Noticing Serb's perplexed expression, Free added, "If that does not yet come naturally to you, think of a moment where you felt uplifted or in bliss. Choose to really feeeeeel it."

Different expression. Same perplexed look. Free elaborated, "Or imagine finding out that your deeply desired wants and wishes just came true."

Better. Expression changed. Energy enhanced. Still perplexed.

Free tried again, "Okay, how about this? Think of the joyful satisfaction you would experience if someone pulled your finger at the perfect time for you to let out the biggest, best feeling, most fulfilling fa—"

"Got it. All makes sense now," groan-chuckled Serb, "So, how's it work?" Serb was excited. He was liking this new version of Godfried.

"Through a copper ring made of crystals. Once it surrounds your thumb, your energy merges with the powers the crystals provide," she added.

"And how do you end it?" Serb asked, ready to give it a go.

"Spin it around once, and then tap the main crystal and you are instantly back to reality. Unless, of course, you chose to imagine your game as the reality.... Then you're in a loop that may never set you free," Free giggled, "Oh yes, very important. There is a *just-in-case* timer, just in case you lose track of time, or nature calls, or you give power to a negative mindset!"

~ 152 ~

"Cool! Can two people play?" Serb asked excitedly as he noticed the count-down timer on the wall.

~ ~ ~

"There's only one seat, Serb. So, nada, definitely not…well, at least not physically," She started to grin, "but, in *game reality*, yes, absolutely, for sure. Why? Because it's all up to you and your imagination. Want someone else? Bring him, her, them all in!" Free replied high-spiritedly.

"Awesome. Can I test it out NOW!?"

"Go for it, I will be up on the main deck in the control area. Have fun. The crystals automatically activate once you are settled into the chair. Place your finger into the ring and sit motionless for eleven seconds while it accesses your brain's thought up thoughts. It may help to meditate first."

With that Free turned and left the room. There were some ship diagnostics she needed to run, so now seemed like a good time to disappear.

Serb walked over to the chair with wonderment. His head was overflowing with ideas of what to play. In between those ideas were a string of, *How cools*! He had actually been thinking those words almost non-stop since he left Author's house which must have been ages ago but was in fact only pages ago.

"OK, I'm ready," he said as he positioned himself.

The chair itself looked like a king's throne. It was wood framed with a lion head carved in its top panel. Serb slid into the chair.

Almost immediately, every ache in his body became enveloped in cushy cushions which made them feel as comfortable as the chair looked. Extending his arms onto the armrests, he felt himself further relax.

"Wow, I can sit here all day, with no desire to get up, eat, talk, workout or use the bathroom." Serb whispered to himself.

~   ~   ~

While deciding on his game play, the ceiling seemed to descend all around him. Serb felt a sort of out-of-body experience taking over. He was entering into *meditation land*, letting it transform his entire being from the inside. It was like his mind left his body to stand in an empty space. No room, no floor, no ceiling, no walls. Just silence, except for the beat of his own heart, to which he then attuned his mind. At that point, all of a sudden, the air melted and collapsed— or something unexplainable happened—and just like that, Serb's scene changed.

Serb was surrounded by a huge rubber-tire-like bubble. Nearby was a ball holder thing. He seemed to be in a gully of some sort with a straightaway that went on so far he couldn't see the end from his vantage point. At the same moment, he could also see everything from a different position, above him. He finally realized what was happening. Pinball, the game he chose. You see, Serb felt that a pinball machine was the safest bet. And it had been a dream of his to do something unique as a pinball player so that he'd get into the *Guinness Book of World Records*. His other considered options included white water rafting or an action-packed shooting game. He knew those could hurt. So being an amazing pinball player, he thought a simple game would be cool. He was so good that without tilting the machine, the machine would tilt. However, since he was unfamiliar with the intricacies of this seating device contraption, he didn't quite remember to visualize the exact perspective he wanted.... So instead of merely playing pinball, he was also being played. He was both the ball *and* the one playing the ball; he was both the machine and the 'ball-banger' known as the flipper. He was each of those things simultaneously. Yes, all at the same time. This was surely going to be quite the experience.

Oh, ishkabibble, he thought.

Then with the follow-up thought of, *Oh well* in his mind, he pulled all the way back on the trigger—um, himself—and let it snap, bracing for the explosion he was going to feel when the ball—also him—was hit.

A rush of air, a thunderous bang, and a jolt that surely would require multiple non-surgical surgery bodywork adjustments, Serb was shot forward from the launching pad. It was the fastest he had ever moved. He braced himself for what surely would be a huge thud off that rubber wall he saw quickly approaching. He watched from above as well, as the ball shot up to the side and smashed through the first turn, past three toll gates, and into the main part of the game. Serb, as the ball, was almost blinded by the array of lights that suddenly became visible after he shot out from the blackness of the tunnel.

Still dizzy from the bump against the wall, Serb felt helpless. He decided to go with the flow, letting whatever was to happen happen, and to be okay with it. That made everything easier. So he aimed towards the middle point-maker which offered the most points: 2,000 in the middle, compared to 350 on the right and 500 on the left. The light tower was also lit up so Serb might be able to earn an extra 500 points! As both the ball and the player, Serb used all his might to make that happen. Rolling at a really fast speed as the ball, he got halfway through the center gate. Suddenly something erupted from the floor, tossing him backwards so unexpectedly that he went for a counterclockwise spin. He thought he must have turned upside down at least 300 times before bouncing off the far wall.

~   ~   ~

The blaring music seemed to echo off every corner, in rhythm with the blinking lights. He couldn't help but dance. He kinda wished he hadn't because it added bumps to the already bumpy ride. Passing more gates, Serb unexpectedly earned an extra 250 points. To congratulate this accomplishment, a cloud of smoke shot out of the floor and up Serb's nose. Barely able to see, and definitely not able to smell, Serb didn't know where to go. But then, just as fast as it arose, the smoke disappeared...revealing much to Serb's dismay that he was speeding right into the flippers at the opening to the pit. Boom! Serb, as the player, hit the buttons at the side of the machine thrusting Serb, as the ball, forward with gusto. Waiting for the flipper to potentially smack him sure was an odd experience. Much to his delight, it turned out to be the best rush he'd ever had. "Yesssss," he screamed (the whole time, in fact— well, up until he shot past the flippers and came to a rest in the dark gully, signifying he struck out).

Catching his breath, Serb conceded that that was enough fun for right now and initiated the closing sequence.

He took in one final deep breath, closed his eyes, and by the time he exhaled he was sitting back in the seating device in the Games Room. He stood up, surprised that he was not dizzy in any way, and so grateful for the opportunity to have played. He then left to locate Free, think up even better games, and gush all about his experience.

CHAPTER TWELVE

NEXT STEPS

"A burger," Orville said out of nowhere.

"Huh?" Serbinand asked. "I heard you mumbling about your hunger so I recommend a burger. Oh ye- ." Before Orville had a chance to finish his *yeah*, Serbinand—whose stomach rumbles confirmed he truly was very hungry—burst out, "So let's do it.... This 'burger' thing is food, right?!"

"Yes. Face-shoveling food. Food that put Jime in a good mood. Food that sure was loved by that dude...who is now you, so you should love it too."

"Sounds good, go on!" Serbinand was intrigued.

Orville, who assumed Serbinand was talking about his singing, continued even though he had nothing more to add, "Face-shoveling food. Face-shoveling foood foood foooooood. Good for your 'tude. Face-shoveling foooood."

"I meant to go on about this burguhhh," Serbinand laughed, no longer contemplating digging into his belly button for the leftover bean-smush.

"Well, let's start with the bread. It's often in my head. Soft, spongy, not sweet...a definite treat. Sometimes it is sprinkled with sesame seeds—I think Jime requested that for meeee. Nice of him too, but no seeds, just bun and burguhhh would do."

"Wait," Serbinand interrupted. "I want to look up burguhh."

"OK, but look up hamburger. It's the same. That's its official name," Orville offered, feeling disappointed as he wanted to describe the mouth-watering image he was picturing in his head.

"What is hamburger," Serbinand asked, unfazed. Then he read it, "The term hamburger originally comes from the German city of Hamburg. In German, *burg* means *castle*. And *burger* describes someone coming from that castle or town. Voila Hamburger!"

"That's it? Bullsit," quipped Orville, realizing that he could better describe this burger his mouth was watering for.

"It is," answered Serbinand, confused, not quite sure he was hungry enough to eat a castle, but still deciding to trust his new friend. "Well, let's get to Hamburg right away!"

"Here's the thing, I must sing" sang Orville, "to let you know that Germany is quite faaar. You can't even get there by car. You would have to fly and go through customs to get by. But when I say fly, I don't mean fly like how I fly, I—"

"Hold up. Wait. Did you say customs?" Serbinand became inquisitive.

"Yup. Yes, correct."

"OK, never mind then. Definitely not worth it. Or is it?!"

Serbinand reminisced, "I once forgot my documents while passing into Garshilang. I was forced to pay a fine and had to spend three days working as a butler for one of the prison wardens. He did have a nice house though, and an *amazing* sauna, which doubled as my hiding spot! Took them the whole three days to find me. Then my service there was done. They gave me a purple apple on my way out. Yeah, that sure was nice, but I got way lost and umm...well, now I'm scared of customs. Oh, and they also have a warrant out for my arrest."

"Back in the day, many Germans chose to emigrate here. So maybe someone from that Hamburg place, became an ace, and opened up a restaurant here where you can order hamburgers, maybe beer." Orville answered with hope, wondering if he even believed himself.

"Back in what day?" Serbinand asked. He missed everything Orville said after that as he was ruminating about what that exactly meant.

"Good question. Random wonderings for the win. I have no clue. Maybe humans do. Just heard it said before. I can't say anymore. Orville slipped into deep thought. "Maybe it doesn't mean squat. Maybe when someone forgot, that's what they thought. Or instead of being specific, they tried to be prolific," a perplexed Orville replied.

"Weird. Okay, whatever day it was, I am now more curious than ever about the taste of a hamburguhh. Just gush to me everything you know."

Yay, thought Orville as he started craving a bite big time, "And it's a hamburger. A ground-up meat formed into a patty—that may or may not be fatty. When cooked it becomes like a loaf, but also not at all like a loaf. It becomes hardish on the outside, if grilling techniques are well applied. It stays softish inside, but not really soft, just not crispy-stuffed. Deelishhh."

Serbinand wasn't too sure that would taste good, but, he reasoned, he was talking to a pretty smart bird, so maybe he should just go for it.

Orville continued singing. It sounded like quite the production—if only he could properly carry the tune, "With burgers you often feel grease. Helps your throat slide it down with ease. Placed in a bun with veggies and cheese. (It's the bright orange cheese that Jime did please.) Only thing is the cheese may give you the farts—or—squirts—or—squirts of farts—or—squirty farts—or—farty squirts—also known as a fart-attack shart-attack. If that happens, you can't hold back. But with regards to slippery poo, or even hard-to-poo poo, that's dairy's gift to you." Orville, um, sang. He carried on, "With the meat so hot, the cheese just melts on the spot. Add ketchup, mustard, lettuce, delicious pickles (sliced), and onions (diced). Then close'r on up...tadahhhh...a hefty hambuuurgahhh...on the spot.

Yup!!" Orville seemed mighty impressed with himself. This was his first ever hamburger recital. And it even had an audience!

Orville was having so much fun that he wanted to continue what he had begun. So, he continued what he had begun and began singing about french fries too. "Oh, and definitely order the fries. Yes, they're fried but I don't think that's why they're called fries. Cuz some of them are now baked which according to Jime are also yum. So, order fries on the side. Preferably the homemade chunky ones—they're wide (rhymes with side). Wait, there's more. You need gravy too. A skinny dip for your fries, even though to you it may now look like a dairy-induced pooooo."

~ ~ ~

Just when Serbinand thought he was done, Orville's tune about burgers and fries, turned into a tune about milkshakes too. So off he sang, not even caring of his self-imposed rhyming rule, "Milkshake, you gotsta get a milkshake. Nope—not simply milk that was shaked. Ice cream (made from milk) that gets shaken with milk—along with other flavors that go well with milk shaked with ice cream so that together they form a shake." Orville also did not care if he made full sense or not. That was fine because Serbinand was in awe.

Suddenly though, something changed. Orville lowered himself to hover by Serbinand's nose. He seemed especially serious. He was about to issue a warning. That's why. It was about milk and milk-related things. "Stomach aches are known to happen, but don't let your mood dampen. Sometimes, when the taste is first rate, inflammation is an accepted bait." He was not done, "At least that's what I observed with Jime…and since you are him, I wanted to fill you in."

What a considerate little flying yellow Orville fellow, thought Serbinand. Before he could think any more, Orville continued, "That aside, time to make your smile wide. The milkshake is sucked through a straw. Yes, it goes up a hole into your jaw. But you first have to suck suck suuuuck, sometimes it takes luck. Before the milk-shaken-with-ice-cream drink came through, Jime's face used to turn blue. But when it finally did and he got what he pleased, guess what happened next? BrainFreeeeeeze!"

Serbinand was the one who seemed confused now. "Why would that be good?"

"Hmm, well, hmmm, I dunno," Orville continued, dumbfounded, "It was hilarious to watch though, y'know? It was like, *wait for it, wait for it…whoa!!*"

Serbinand did know. He remembered a time back when he watched a *Three's Company* clip where Jack actually sucked a milkshake up his nose. His wide-eyed reaction made the entire studio audience laugh, as if on cue. *I bet it was from the brainfreeze,* he thought. Then on second thought he realized it wasn't *Three's Company* where that happened. It was a dream.

Getting hungrier, Serbinand announced, "That sounds amazing. I'm willing to try it. We need to find this type of food, stat!" He added, "I apologize for doing a web search before consulting with you. Your words actually made it so there is nothing else I want to fill my mouth with, not even candied bruggs," Serbinand gushed.

"Got it! *We B Bergerrzzz,*" Serbinand read after asking his screen to disclose the ultimate burger place, "*Home of the most delicious burger'.*" He seemed pleased, specifically because the radar signal indicated that the only direction they needed to go was straight. "Six hours by foot."

"That works for me. Only I'll fly, high." giggled Orville.

THE RIDICULOUS

So Serbinand and Orville started out. They didn't even look back at the baked bean remnants, vomit, and very confused cow animal that they left behind (in Chapter 7, you will recall, Signed Author).

~ ~ ~

Serb returned to the main control area where he found Free dancing in what looked like a state of bliss. She surely was lovely. He still couldn't believe this was all real. *Guess the manifestation practices I dabbled in actually paid off!* he thought, reflecting on his experience. *I'm on a spaceship…with a 'Happy Room'! I'm able to play virtual reality games that seem more real than virtual; I have the ability to go anywhere, and do anything I think; And then, there's FREE.* She alone convinced him of his powers to manifest his heart's desires and dreams.

With that thought still finding pleasure in his mind, he was aroused by the touch of a kiss on his cheek. "Wow. Nice timing!" Serb exclaimed. "What was that for?" he asked confused, yet full of enthusiasm and joy.

"I knew you'd smile," Free said with a smirk. "Now wake up from your haze. I've done all I need to do here. Let's go do something fun, together!"

That was just what Serb needed to hear. "What are our options?"

"Well, that is a huge question," answered Free. "What would bring you joy? I ask because everything is possible. Besides, choosing to get clear with what your heart truly desires, allows you to enjoy your experience so much more, don'tcha think?"

"I agree. Good point." Serb announced out loud.

"To figure it out, I suggest you download an insight. To invite it in, simply focus on your breathing. Take a *breath-break* so to speak and create your own perfect space of stillness. Then let your mind go free," Free explained. "Something neat will pop in. Whatever that is, let's do it."

"Definitely. I'm game." And then on second thought, he said, "But not right now, later. I'm a little too excited right now. I feel like I can't stand still."

~   ~   ~

"Got it. Ecstatic dance for the win!" exclaimed Free.

"Ecstatic dance, you say? You've got to be kidding me. I've heard so much about it, and how it can help free your mind. I nixed it because, well, being ecstatic, that probably needs a lot of energy," Serb chuckled. Then he added, "AND I don't dance".

"Well now you will. Ecstatic dance coming right up! Shall we end it with a meditative *breath-break* and see if any downloads come on in about what to do next?"

"Yes. Meditation all the way!" Serb exclaimed, surprised that he actually felt ecstatic—he knew he must now dance—it must be her energy, or something.

Free lowered the lights in their immediate section. Smoke was ignited, and the mist machines did their job to fill the air. Psychedelic lights sparked up. Free kicked off her sandals in anticipation. As soon as they hit the far wall with a thud, ecstatic dance music exploded into the room. It was as if she cued it with her feet. Halt. Is that even possible?

The sound was so loud *and* so quiet. The floor somehow swayed with the vibrations of the beat. It was as if a dance floor opened up right under his feet. It did. Serb recalled his self-promise and recognized that as his cue. *Oh wait, I don't recall that, or do I? Can it be Serbinand's thoughts that were coming through? Is that possible?* Either way, dancing was calling his name.

When the music got to its peak, Free activated the *Floor Changers*, turning the solid surface into bouncy-tramampoline material. Serb let the rhythm take control. He was still getting used to his new bodysuit, so this was an opportune time to test its limits. He went with it and began thrashing his arms around, circling his booty, and shaking his head all in time with the melody. Yes, he may have looked odd, but it felt so awesome that he just didn't care. *Hmmm. So, this is dancing*, he thought, as a huge smile took control of his face. *I never thought I'd like it, but I do. It's so freeing...I feel so good.*

He felt the musical notes transfer right through into his being, energizing his entire body. He experienced sound vibrations from his head to his feet, from his feet to his head, and even inside…continually, again and again.

In the simple shift of a moment, he then found himself lying beside Free, listening to the words of a Sound Shaman. With eyes closed, they were then guided to visualize the notes as colors. Soon they were deep in a meditative trance. Much to Serb's desire, Free's fingers actually touched his. It happened just as he was visualizing a wave of love energy pouring out from his heart space, showering light on everything within 91.4 meters of his vicinity. How sweet!

"Wow, that was powerful," he breathed. "What did you see?"

"You. You were listening to music on a beach and dancing *free* style (pun not intended, but then intended once I realized it was a pun). Later you performed on a stage with a hula-hoop, flower sticks and some sort of torch. It was part of a body empowerment event or something…? I was just sitting back, watching the creative way you were expressing yourself. You looked absolutely beautiful. I loved watching you dance when you closed your eyes and just let go. You were wearing a white hippie shirt with frills on it that showed me you have a belly button ring. I saw it as you spun around…"

"Yes, I know exactly what you saw. You are talking about a *Schuzzpppluzz Festival*. Well done on the download. This festival attracts people from all galaxies of intelligence who wish to celebrate themselves for at least a few minutes, (up to a month). There is actually a *Schuzzpppluzz Festival* taking place right now!

So, if you want to live out that vision, we can be there faster than you say yes—"

"Yeess—"

~   ~   ~

They headed out near the edge of highway number eleven. They walked past trees and huge, towering rocks, leaving footprints in the grass and mud that marked their tracks. The seasons were still changing, which turned out to be good for their venture. It meant mosquitos were weeks away from claiming the region as their own. While the sun shined hot waves of heat, the breeze added to the ambiance, making for a comfortable trek along the Muskoka highway.

The entire region sat on a shield of rock that dated back to the time period when the planet was formed. The area was also covered with forest. A mixture of trees—hardwood: maple, birch, oak; and coniferous: white and red pine, tamarack, and hemlock— lined the highway. They were swaying and seemed happy to be doing their job well. Some were still bare from the winter. Others were lying on the ground, resting from the effects of storms that had made their way through. *It must take muscle to hold up all that snow and ice. I guess tiredness overcame the ones that didn't choose to work out in the off-season,* Serbinand reasoned in his head. As a form of farewell, he stopped at each fallen branch and sent a message of gratitude, offering well wishes for their life's next adventures. He pictured white light shining down on the lot of them, sending them a request to keep up with their exercises. *You never know when the need should arise to flex your muscles,* Serbinand told them through his internal head-speak. He then thought, *"Wow, this is new!"* and became graciously impressed with his new personality that for some reason Author had brought through.

Birds were chirping at them as they made their way. Between the birdies and the rush of cars, Serbinand felt he was in a parade. This made him feel special. He stopped quite often to wave and pose, and he'd fling his arms wildly when cars honked. Orville, on the other hand, had no real idea why Serbinand would stop, break into a smile, wave and stare as though he just didn't care. He soon chose to assume

Serbinand was just...practicing his burger order and subsequent happy dance. Satisfied, Orville then joined the birds, and sang amongst them, happy and free as can be.

After passing a few gas stations, and what looked like an awesome candy shop—which was closed—they arrived at *We B Bergerrzzz*. Well, on the wrong street side. In good news, there was a bridge.

"We need to have a chit chat, stat." Orville stated upon realizing that they can't have a conversation in front of people.

"OK, what's up?"

"Well, you see…. You don't know how to do things here without me. But, how should I put this? Hmmm….have you heard? Bird's the word. I. Am. A. Bird.

"So?" Serbinand interrupted.

"It would look odd for us to talk 'n' walk. Most humanoids don't know they can talk to animals too, so it's better to keep our public talks silent between me and you," Orville beautifully splurged out. "That, and, well…Jime asked me to keep it a secret…so, there ya go, yo." Orville's voice sounded especially off key upon realizing the importance of their convo.

Serbinand didn't quite catch on though. It was like his stomach went on pause and his heart took over. "A secret? Why not be proud of the powers he possessed?" beamed Serbinand sensing how fortunate he was to now possess them too.

I'm liking this version of Jime 2.0…whoa, thought Orville but said, "Snap out of it, will ya? We need to have an Aha! What you said is true but not the topic we need to speak through. At least not right

~ 170 ~

now. Now we need some chow. So, we need to figure something out, and proceed without a doubt! But waaahhhhtt??!" After posing that question, a solution almost immediately downloaded in. Orville knew exactly what to do. "I'm going to sit on your shoulder and quietly guide you through. That means I will whisper in your ear. You then repeat everything you hear," Orville belted out, then added in a warning tone "Also, nod your head and smile. We may be there for a while. And if you wish to chat, do not dare, it may cause people to stare!"

"Sure thing! It's Adventure tiiiiiiimmme! Let's do it!" Serbinand yelled. People were staring.

They walked over the bridge, despite a tremendous amount of fear that crept in. The story Orville heard is that people would do anything for a *We B Bergerrzzz* burger, even if it meant dodging speeding cars to get to the other side. In order to keep their customers alive, *We B Bergerrzzz* sprung for this highway overpass instead…or is it an underpass? I guess it depends on who is asking the question, the walkers over top or the drivers beneath. Now that is a rather random wondering. Either way, both Serbinand and Orville were delighted at the sheer terror they felt as the cars zoomed by on the highway below. Orville had flown down to the railing to feel the vibrations too. "*Frogger*! It's like the cars are coming right at you, but at least we're up top and safe," exclaimed Serbinand, kinda scared for his life, and kinda having the most fun he'd had since outmaneuvering the beetles. Orville was enjoying himself too. They stayed like that for a while until they couldn't take the scariness anymore.

Once across, they walked through a parking lot, between a yellow car and a red car, beside a minivan looking for a spot, behind a big red tractor, and around two monster trucks. Just beyond that, they spotted the restaurant's door. Finally.

Stepping into the narrow and quite crowded order zone, they were immediately greeted by someone ready to take their meal request. *Efficient*, thought Serbinand.

"What'r you have?"

"What do you suggest?" Serbinand responded.

"Good one, well done" Orville whispered in his ear, impressed he thought that up himself.

"I would go with the cheeseburger, fully dressed, french fries with gravy, and a chocolate shake."

"Then that's what I will have."

The order-taker scribbled a few things on a piece of paper, then left.

As soon as she was gone, a new person appeared. He asked Serbinand for $27.32. Fortunately, the wads of cash he pulled out from his sack covered it. He even got some bills back. He worked hard stuffing those in his pocket so as to ensure he had them for later use. That took longer than the order. *Hmm. This seems archaic. I bet this currency thing will become obsolete*, thought Serbinand.

Success! They got their food. Other than the ketchup-mustard-gravy mishap, Orville didn't even need to help, much.

They stepped outside and headed to one of the wooden picnic tables reserved for eaters of the food.

~ ~ ~

"Klorsherdukk", Serbinand cheered! He was ready to face-shovel the burger all in. But first he had to smell it. So he did. Yum. Ready for the first bite, he closed his eyes, bit down, focused his attention and enjoyed each morsel of his chew. He picked out each texture and temperature as it passed by his lips, touched his teeth, and flowed over his tongue. He tasted the juices as the deliciousness broke down within his cheeks. A party was happening right there in his mouth.

With a bit of burger lodged securely between his front teeth, Serbinand dipped fry after fry into the steaming hot bowl of brown gravy.

"Wow, this is good. This is great," he spoke aloud to Orville, no longer caring if people thought he was still playing talksie with himself.

He reached for the chocolate shake to cool down his throat. It was exactly like Orville described. Another deep suck in through the straw and still nothing…until…pooofff! Suddenly soft, cold, creamy, and oh-so-chocolatey yumminess filled his mouth. Then just as suddenly, it got swallowed down, much to Serbinand's delight. And no brain freeze. He was in luck.

"That was awesome…do it again! You seem to be in heaven's zen." Orville tweeted.

"Being a good shake sucker must be another one of my gifts!" To demonstrate, Serbinand took another sip. Feeling quite special to have his own flying cheerleader, he placed a piece of burger on his shoulder. He felt that would be less conspicuous than holding out a bite. He then offered, "Want some? Come eat."

Serbinand and Orville sat in silence for what seemed like a bliss-filled eternity enjoying their food, sharing their food, laughing all along the way, and of course, making noises from different openings in their bodies.

"So, what's it made of, anyway?" Serbinand wondered and asked out loud.

"Not sure. Either it's pure or something that could make you hurl. Sometimes it may be better not to check, blech. But if you prefer, I'll concur. Go give it a whirl."

"Okay. Let's start with the french fries," Serbinand decided and looked it up. "Fried elongated pieces of potatoes, hmmm."

"Ok, here we go. What's a *potato?*" responded the bird.

"Says here it's some kind of vegetable that grows in the ground. Sounds like magic. Must be a treat."

"Yeah, a treat to eat. Ok, great, but what about milkshake?"

"A frothy drink made of cold milk." Now Serbinand took control and continued searching without being prompted, "Milk, a liquid secreted by a cow. What's a cow? Cow, a..."

"Wait, I know that one...oh what fun," chirped Orville, laughing, "Remember being a viewer to the 'mooer'? The animal that didn't yield and kicked you clear across the field?"

THE RIDICULOUS

~ ~ ~

"The one eating grass?"

"No yo, the other thing that didn't yield and kicked you clear across the field! Alas, of course, the one eating grass!" mocked Orville, mis-assuming he would come across as funny.

"You are starting to sound like Godfried."

"Sorry.... Wow. Yes, that was a cow." Orville lowered his head feeling somewhat ashamed. After all, Serbinand was so nice.

"Wait. How do cows turn grass into this amazing chocolate liquid?" "Just like you, I have no clue," Orville admitted.

"Ok, next. Hamburger - a sandwich consisting of a cooked round patty of ground or chopped beef. Let's look up beef...OK ...Beef...AHHHHH!" Serbinand screamed as he jumped out of his chair.

"Oh oh...have a seat...What did we eat?" asked Orville confused. "A cow! A cow! We ate a moooooooooomooooooo!"

"We ate a cowwwwwww?! WoW!" At this point Orville's singing had gotten pretty bad, reflecting how he must feel.

"How can something so cute—although with a nasty temper—be so tasty? I will tell you something. The next time I see a cow, I am going to show it such respect, especially if it doesn't kick me. I will even forgive it and kiss it. This was one of the tastiest meals I ever ate. It was great. Them cows, they should be revered!"

~ ~ ~

"What are the odds? In a country called India, they are treated like gods," Orville concurred.

"To cows everywhere: Thank you for this amazing food you have given me!" Serbinand declared. He turned to Orville and asked, "How do they get rewarded?"

"Rewarded?"

"Yea, for giving such a wonderful gift. Surely, they must get a significant reward or some riches to live an amazing life!"

"You would think so. But I have no idea, though. Jime hadn't shared that with me, y'see," replied Orville.

"Well, they certainly deserve our respect." With that, Serbinand granted it respect. He then stood up rather abruptly and burped. This signaled that he was done. With that he decided it was time to move his legs and figure out where they should take him to adventure next.

Heading back down the highway, with little talk, the duo had no plan. Zero. Upon leaving, an awesome song was playing on the radio. It was coming out of one of the parked cars. *"Sign, sign, everywhere a sign"*. Upon hearing it, they decided this was a sign to watch for signs. Not wanting to miss such a sign, they chose to be on the lookout. The first sign they saw was an actual sign, *"Moose Crossing."* They didn't know how that would help, but they decided to stop and wait for the moose to cross anyway.

CHAPTER THIRTEEN

GODFRIED'S TURN

Somewhere way down the circuit highway in Godfried's belly of signals, beeps, bends and modern-day unconsciousness, something gargantuan was about to happen. According to the official *Recorders of Unusual Occurrences*, a little spark went off. To some it was just a tiny "pop". For Godfried though, it was the opening to an entire new awakening…an awakening for which he was to assume control. It was as if something somewhere even deeper, deep inside him was further waking him up out of his fog. "It's my time now!" it seemed to shout inside Godfried's circuit-filled head. Huh?

While the "Free" part of me is out gallivanting as a human, and Serbinand is roaming planet Earth, I am going to enjoy my ME time too, Godfried justified.

"Let's do this!" he yelled, loudly—like he was getting ready for battle—to no one in particular, and for no apparent reason.

A wave of flashback memories exploded in his mind. He was reminded of one of the crazy adventures he had with Serbinand and friends many, many years ago. They had all eaten some "magic cookies". Well, that's what the guy at the street concert said, and he did look like he knew what he was talking about, especially when it came to magic. After all, he was wearing a *Grateful Dead* shirt and it was quite psychedelic. After eating a few or more - they were delicious—Serbinand, Bernard, Dantow, and Godfried—in the form of his Portable Extension Tech unit, otherwise known as PET back then—headed down to the outdoor adventure water slide park, which was closed. There was a big fence around it. This was not ideal. It proved to be only one of their obstacles that night. *Let's do this!* they all had thought seemingly in unison.

PET only entered their life four minutes before. It was a grand prize awarded to both him and Serbinand for winning the *Simondians Galactic Twisto Race.*

PET had four legs for walking, running, climbing and stalking, and was quite capable of moving on his own. Its mainframe was covered in soft fur, well…soft, until the need to protect its innards was triggered. If that happened, each strand of fur instantaneously morphed into a sharp spike.

With the park closed, *this was the best place to test PET's abilities, surely,* Godfried recalled thinking. *Somehow we need to get in.* Everyone, including PET, looked at the fence, held their breath, repeated, "Let's do this" (only this time out loud), sucked in their bellies and decided to go for it. Shrinking their body like that, they were able to easily squeeze their way through the fence, sideways.

Once inside, they had an excellent view of the park, including the security guards patrolling the grounds.

~ ~ ~

The guards were getting closer and closer…and then turned around and walked away. Perfect. Time to play.

Thanks to the giant "You Are Here" map, they knew exactly where they were. Which also meant they knew exactly where to go. Off they went, only to arrive at the coolest place in the park… oh yeah…*Rope Kingdom*!

That place was all sorts of awesome. Bridges made only of ropes connected tower after tower, each with its own color-coded flag. Ladders led right to the top. Safety nets stretched out below. The only thing missing was ambience. During park hours, music could be heard throughout the kingdom. Its vibrations could also be felt inside one's body, making the ropes course that much more enjoyable. Sure, PET could have conjured up the same playlist. However, noise, especially that loud, would surely have alerted park patrol, and likely quite quickly. So, they had each chosen a tower and agreed to race to the top in silence. That's when things had turned "magical".

Serbinand's mind morphed into *Game-Time-Awareness* mode. He had been determined to be the first one to the top. Winning surely would come with years of bragging rights, possibly even decades. The winner would even get to keep that tower's flag. So, it was definitely worth it.

Satisfied he had mentally prepared himself, Serbinand looked at his friends then yelled, "GO!" They had all jumped forward…and…well, let's leave the exact details of the race for another time. For the purpose of this story though, just know that

Serbinand won. To celebrate, they all ran to the *Sky High Scenic Tower*. This tower looked out above all the other towers. Although it was dark, they could tell the ropes there were even bigger...as was the net. It was supersized. Serbinand decided that meant it would be fun to jump on to. So off he went. He jumped from the tower's balcony and aimed for the net. When he landed, he realized that maybe this net was not designed to be jumped into. It felt less like a net, and more like an iron shield. His sides, legs, head, and arms were actually yelling at him for treating them so horribly.

"How was it?" Dantow had called down.

"Awesome!" Serbinand had replied, accompanied by a thumbs up sign. Next, Dantow had plummeted down. He also landed hard and immediately realized Serbinand had tricked him. His body needed a few minutes to be still while it tried to reverse what just happened. He needed it to readjust.

"OK...good one.... Let's get Bernard," Dantow whispered to Serbinand, after he was readjusted, while waving Bernard down. "It's awesome," Dantow shouted.

"No way! That looks like it could be painful. For all I know, you guys feel the hurt and want me to feel it too." Turns out, the magic cookies had made Bernard extra smart. "If it's so much fun, I want to see both of you do it again. If you do, I will join you."

Serbinand and Dantow knew exactly what to do. They climbed all the way back up the rope maze. Afraid of laughing, and trying not to think of their impending pain, they both jumped as soon as they got to the top.

As promised, Bernard followed suit and landed with a thud. Pretending not to care, he said he had known it was a trick all along and just wanted to share in the story which was bound to be told. Laughing it off, they all decided to encourage PET to do it too. And that's where things had gotten more than a little out of hand.

What an excellent way to test out their new PET, Serbinand heard himself think on repeat. In retrospect that must have been his way to convince himself it was safe to ignore his intuition that clearly was saying not to let it happen.

Then, it was PET's turn. "Let's do this!!" PET screamed. No one expected what happened next. PET had taken a running start, and leaped off the edge! Being his first time doing something of this nature, his thoughts went full into panic mode. This, of course, activated the spikes that enveloped his body.

When he landed, he ripped right through the rope net, and then proceeded to slice through a wooden beam. This created a series of chaotic events. Who knew that the *non-net* net that was catching them was also the support system for that entire complex!? Within a second or less, it was raining ropes, planks, flags, and ladders everywhere they turned.

What to do? Run! But first they had to release PET, who was tangled in the center of it all. To do that they had to somehow calm him down so that his fur would come back. After an intense moment, a song, quite a few nicks, and one pint of blood, PET easily removed himself off the pillar, screaming joyfully the entire time.

Now, you can imagine the amount of noise this little fiasco created. Of course, the security patrol team was on their way. "Run!"

Dantow yelled. But they couldn't. *Rope Kingdom* had very specific rules: "*please remove your shoes*" which they had already done. Made sense at the time. But when they went back to retrieve them, they got caught.

There was no way security could hassle them...they too were laughing hard! Mocking them, actually. "Tee-hee-hee. Caught for breaking and entering, and destroying everything all because they respected the 'please remove your shoes' rule." Security continued laughing for the rest of their time together and advised them to escape back through the fence from which they came. So not only was it one of Godfried's and Serbinand's most exciting life experiences, they were actually let go without any fines. Following that, *Rope Kingdom* was closed forever. A suspected localized tornado. At least that's what the sign said. As rumor has it, the security guards then told the story over and over in many different ways for years and years to come.

~   ~   ~

Wow, that surely was a long interlude. Hope you enjoyed it. Now back to the story. (Signed, Author.)

~   ~   ~

"Let's do this" Godfried said again, re-inspired by his memory that he could do wrong and not get caught, and have the time of his life too. So, he decided to scan the local announcement boards to see what might be really cool to do. He was hoping for a race, an obstacle course, or something even more thrilling...and potentially dangerous. *Bienfang. Bienfang, that's it!*

Godfried realized that in order to get to Bienfang, he may need to take control of this story. This was a very different plot than the one Author had intended, so there may be repercussions. He had to think long and hard about how he could accomplish his plan in the most effective way.

"It's. My. Time. Now!" he bellowed, with a force seeming to shake the very fabric of time.

~ ~ ~

The next thing Serb knew, he was walking in the middle of a mythical forest. Free was standing next to him. They were holding hands. Their legs were walking them down a path blanketed with trees on both sides. A canopy of leaf-lined branches hung overhead, although some were only partially dressed. Autumn. It was so magnificent that Serb could actually hear flutes playing *Jethro Tull* tunes in his head. Or was that coming from somewhere else? He wasn't sure.

"This is awesome," he cheered as they continued past the shrubs, trees, and fallen branches.

"I hope you like the colors," Free said with a sweet smile.

They slowed down to take in the scenery and forest bathe. Covered with leaves that had already fallen, the ground was now interwoven with colors and patterns, beautiful as art. Off to the left, was a lake sparkling with sunlight. Beyond that, rolling hills. Magical.

As they rounded the next corner, unusual light rays caught them by surprise, causing their eyes to widen in astonishment, while still squinted. Weird. These were colors Serb was pretty sure he had never seen, nor even knew existed. All the while the music Serb had heard seemed to be getting louder. Maybe it wasn't in his head?

"What's going on?" Serb spoke, mesmerized by his senses. *Is this the Schuzzpppluzz Festival,* he wondered, feeling very uncertain—and uncomfortable—about what he was actually seeing.

~ ~ ~

"Did you see that?" Serbinand shrilled. "What? A moose on the loose?" Orville asked.

They had been standing in the same spot for what seemed to be hours. With that much time on their hands, they wagered a bet on how many moose would burst through the trees to cross the street. Whoever was furthest from the real count would owe the other a favor—anything at all—to be redeemed at any time, upon request. Serbinand thought 2,009 was the right number, and Orville pegged it at 18.

The whole bet wagering was Serbinand's idea. In his youth on Placellner he lost many bets to Godfried who usually responded with "I reserve the right to favor-request whenever and as often as I feel like it." Sometimes it would be years after the incident. This time, Serbinand wanted to win and be in control.

"Nope, that was not a moose. Actually, I don't even know what a moose looks like. And I doubt a moose would be crossing the street as streaks of off-black colored lights filling the sky with illogical shades," Serbinand explained.

"Well, do you think the moose will ever cross? Maybe not, if Author is their boss!" Orville smirked, even though he was getting impatient.

"I don't know. I don't think the moose have anything to do with this. I just have such a weird gut feel about what I just witnessed. Yet, y'know, it seems like I have seen all this before.... Only maybe it was in a dream, or movie...or—"

"Well, let's each face a different direction and keep watch on our own section," Orville suggested, cutting Serbinand off, clearly bored by the conversation.

~ ~ ~

"Okay. Except I'm going to put my spin on." *When in doubt make spins and see what happens* is a saying he remembered from his youth on Placellner. He figured this would allow him to take in the scenery and be on the lookout for moose crossers, or those wildly weird flashes of lights. "Why don't you go for a fly-around through that area while I spin out right here?" Serbinand pointed.

~ ~ ~

"Ok. Hope you don't get vertigo. Off I go." "Vertigo?"

~ ~ ~

"Look it up, look it up, look it upppp," Orville chanted. And with that he flew off.

Remembering how each word just led to another word, which

led to another word, which led to his discovery about the fate of his grass-eating friend, Serbinand decided that he would not look it up at all. Instead, he would just begin spinning…and see what happens.

He took his knapsack off first, ruffled through its contents and discovered the piece of chocolate that Jime had packed. It looked similar to a treat back home, so he was excited to taste the Earth version. *Ummmm…ummmm…yyyummm,* he thought as the bite melted in his mouth.

He returned the rest of this morsel of deliciousness back into the container before gently placing the knapsack under the Moose Crossing sign. Slowly, he began to shuffle his feet in a rhythmic fashion. He decided to increase the spin speed after each third revolution. By the time he got to thirty, he was in full throttle mode, and the ground seemed to be dancing and swaying all around him.

Suddenly, it felt as if his legs were on *backwards* and he was losing the ability to stand upright. A wobbly feeling overtook his entire being. That's when the nausea kicked in. Serbinand recognized this exact feeling from his binge drinking days. Back then, he would wake up—usually from the floor—not naked, with strange drawings on his eyelids. The exact details are best to be avoided, for everyone's sake. They are quite graphic. Peppermint tea always seemed to do the trick of abating that nausea feeling. At this very moment, though, that certainly was not an option.

Then the ringing in his ears began. It grew louder and louder as he kept up the pace. Next came the twitching, itching, and eye spasms which lasted until his thirty-ninth spin. Serbinand found this all quite entertaining, which pushed him to continue forward. If only the headache hadn't kicked in. It started pounding from the inside out, as if to scream *Let me out of here*. Through many harrowing facial expressions, he managed to get past that feeling too.

Sweating, double vision, and loss of coordination took over. His brain, which couldn't make much sense of his erratic foot movements, decided to let him know and threw him off-balance completely. Just like that—similar to a spinning top spinning out of control, he was out of control. Both legs gave out. He was then flung to a smash landing, once again hitting the grass. This time not even landing that figure eight, or anything close to it. That's when he understood he had pushed it just a wee bit too far.

While fun for a moment, Serbinand realized maybe it would have been an activity best to have been avoided. He decided next time he would take the few moments and look up the meaning from word to word. As he rolled himself over to get up, a rather loud burp escaped his mouth. It came with drool and a spittle of brown liquid, "Yuuummm, chocolate to the rescue." He grinned as he tasted it one last time before it dripped from his lips and splashed onto the ground.

~ ~ ~

The first time Godfried was introduced to Bienfang was when he was not allowed to join Serbinand on one of his adventure-trips with Dantow and Bernard. He followed them instead, using his flying viewing sensor.

This particular trip they had gone to the Jetson's mansion on the peninsula of Horvarth Island, off Lunar Signus. They had been gifted the place for a long weekend so they loaded their ship with essentials like food, dragonweed, a piano, music, clothes, and more food. It had been the cold season, so they brought extra outerwear too, hoping to stay warm.

The music was blaring, and snacks were already being chomped on by the time they arrived. The area had been blanketed in white powder, whose job seemed to be to reflect the sun. It did it so well that goggles were advised. Well, for the Placellners anyway.

The estate's main cabin had five wings to it. The middle section belonged to the masters of the family, and the others belonged to each of their children. Serbinand's group had been given the furthest section of the cottage, closest to the frozen lake. To get there they had to walk through the huge Harworthian room where the ceilings were more than three times the height of Godfried's ship. On the left wall was a chair that was really big. It was a soft purple color, with ninety-one blue lines of pattern. It appeared aged yet really comfy, and cheerfully overlooked the largest fireplace they had ever seen: a wall of four hundred and twenty red bricks and two dozen gray ones that stretched right up to the ceiling. It looked way too big for one Serbinand. It would be more suitable for five of him, as long as they were stacked high upon themselves. On the far-right side there had been a stack of over seventy-five trases, from small kindling pieces to hard, slow-burning ones.

~   ~   ~

Thanks for taking the time out of your reading to read this. Please know that it wasn't my plan to interrupt the beautiful description I was writing in the paragraph above this one. It's just that I had an 'Aha!' moment, and I felt I had to share. You see, after describing the room, and then looking up at the fireplace, I realized I was not clear. Not clear at all. Like, why would Serbinand be stacked on top of himself? He doesn't even have any twins, so there aren't five of him. Well, maybe in another dimension, but I'm not writing about that, I'm writing about this. So, I can definitely improve in my storytelling ways. I had also shared that there were specific things on the left and specific things on the right. But, that, my friends, is not necessarily accurate. Well, it is only if I had shared with you the direction I was facing. Because let's face it…If I was facing backwards, left would be on the opposite side than if I was facing frontwards. Right? (Or do I mean *left*?... Get it?)

Oh, and then there's the issue of the word trases. What is that? Even I had to look it up. It definitely wasn't what I planned to say. It means "after" translated from Spanish. And it wasn't even written in Spanish. Turns out, the word I meant to say was "hearth", as in a rack for wood.

Thinking this through, I guess I could have just changed the wording around without anyone knowing. Too late. Ok, wait, I will. That makes sense, right? Just redo it? While I am at it, maybe I'll use less numbers in the next version, even though they're written out in text. It's just that it seems kinda strange to have put in that many numerical measurements. So, I'll tend to that too.

By the way, I think chortling, which I introduce in Chapter 3 in relation to the crushed ants, is like snorting on top of your laughter. I remember learning that while playing *Balderdash* once, and that's exactly what I did.

Only my mouth was filled with liquid, and yes, the person across from me got a little wet.

Okay. We are ready. Here it is: Take Two. And please note, I changed almost all of it, kind of. Let's start from "Serbinand's group", which was a few sentences into paragraph four. (Signed, Author).

~ ~ ~

Serbinand's group had been given the cabin furthest from civilization, closest to the serenity of the frozen lake. They'd walked into a huge Harworthian room with the ceilings stretching well beyond the height of the ship. The ceilings stretched so high that, for the safety of all necks, it was advised not to look up to the top. On the far side sat a massive chair. It looked big enough for half a dozen people to sit on, all at the same time...without touching. It had been a soft purple color, with blue lines of pattern. Aged and appearing to be really comfy, the couch overlooked the largest fireplace that probably ever existed. Bricks had lined its wall, stretching all the way up to the ceiling. On one side there'd been a rack of wood—*a hearth*—holding tree choppings of all shapes and sizes, from kindling fire starters to large slow-burners, which makes fire watching extra mesmerizing.

~ ~ ~

So, how was that? I know, I changed more than I expected. I hope you enjoyed the revision. I just felt it had to be done. Especially after I re-read the original. Now back to the story.

(Signed, Author).

THE RIDICULOUS

~ ~ ~

Next to the couch had been the kitchen zone. That's where they'd unloaded most of their stuff. After a few snacks of their own, and a welcoming round of dragonweed, they each chose a bedroom and unpacked. Godfried hadn't had anything to unpack, and he had not needed a room in which to sleep. The fact remained that no one knew he was there. So he just hung out overlooking the kitchen, the one place where all people eventually come to congregate.

Finally, the other three emerged, each wearing what they referred to as their relaxo clothes, which must have been why they had turned up the music.

Within minutes there'd been a knock at the door, and the property caretaker—later to be referred to as the Baysville Witch—walked in. She had looked wise, with a hint of mystique. Kinda like the abandoned hotel that banked the property. What a nice surprise it was when she later invited them all back to her cottage for hot chocolate and treats. And of course, Bienfang.

~ ~ ~

WHOOOSSHSHHHHHHHHH!

"*AAHHH, what was that?*" I, Author, asked. I was a bit stunned being pulled away from my writings in that type of haste. And during a flashback moment, too. One of my favorites.

So….What gives? What's going on? WHOOOSSHSHHHHHHHHH! Crash! Boom!

~ 191 ~

~ ~ ~

"That was lit! I see it. I see it," Orville chirped excitedly. But soon he wasn't so sure he should be excited. Explosions of reddish color, then blueish with yellowish, followed by reddish colors again suddenly intertwined with black and off-black, and then everything went colorless. There was nothing for an instant, followed by some kind of insane explosion. That was loud. A moment later, it happened again.

His hopes of getting Serbinand to notice were completely useless. No matter how loud he shrieked or how animated he waved his wings, Serbinand was preoccupied and oblivious. Doing what? Orville was not so sure. It looked like Serbinand was just winding himself up to launch into flight. Getting dizzy just by watching, Orville decided to make a run, umm, fly for it and explore the exploding explosions all on his own.

~ ~ ~

Godfried, still on a high from repeatedly and randomly shouting "*Let's Do It*" and "*It's My Time Now,*" was creating his own powerful wave of energy. Static charges bounced all around his circuitry. At first, it felt amazing, freeing, powerful, and then it changed....

Bright colors, illuminating flashes of non-dazzling colors created dazzlement. The occasional shrieking sounds suddenly exploded all around. This seemed to create a whole new level of existence. Or consciousness, Godfried thought. *No...new levels of POWER,* Godfried realized. "Absolute Power!" This he said out loud.

Orville reached the point closest to the lights. They were shifting quicker now, and he heard the explosions getting louder and louder. *Why weren't the other people more frantic? What is this antic?!"* he frantically thought. It was as if no one seemed to notice anything. That means that....

"Something's wrong," Free breathed. "Something is happening to the ship, or the control system or something.... Something is happening to the ship, or the control system or something.... Something is...."

What. Is. Going. On. Author thought, or wrote, or conjured up, or...

BOOM! BANG!! BOOM!!!

"Hello... It worked. OK, so now that I have *all* of your attention.... Hello. This is Godfried."

Godfried, now in control of the situation, did something really unusual. With a simple, clear and focused thought, he brought everyone back together, but this time into a space of no-space. Serb, Free, Serbinand, and Orville felt they were nowhere, in no-time, as no one, in no-place.

Just potential energy waiting for something to happen.

"If anyone is going to interrupt the story with something meaningful to say, it should be me!" Godfried added.

[*Wait, is his point that it's not ME who can interrupt?* I, Author, am wondering.]

"What are you talking about?" Serbinand asked, concerned about what might be going on. He knew what Godfried was capable of doing.

"Talking about? I'm talking about *Sir Author* jumping in and stealing my thunder…and yours…and yours…and yours!"

[*My gosh, he is,* I, Author, suddenly realized.]

"Huh?" Serbinand was confused. "It was one meeting we had, that's it. And it all worked out… We all got to dream up one amazing wish. And that wish came true. We got what we wanted."

"Wrong. I know everything. I *am* the master computer after all. That means *I* know what has actually been written. Embedded among the words, paragraphs, and chapters, Author actually interrupts often, and never asks permission. It's a total disruption to my system. And he is getting in the way of my fans!" Godfried bellowed.

"You mean his side stories and flashbacks?" Free asked, not seeming perturbed at all.

~ ~ ~

~ 194 ~

"Yes, those. Exactly!" shrieked Godfried, "I have had enough. It's *my* turn now!"

"You knew about the other interruptions?" Serb turned to Free, letting Godfried's voice drone on in the background.

"Of course, I did. I'm still Godfried, in some way. And I rather enjoy Author's interjections. I think it adds to the story, you know. Definitely makes it more interesting, at least from my perspective."

"OK, so let me know if I have this right," started Serb addressing Godfried, "It was you who somehow caused those big bangs and non-color color explosions I saw?" Serb could tell he was right just by the energy emanating off the smug look on Godfried's non-existent face. "And whatever you did broke you out of Author's control, didn't it?"

"Ding, ding, ding!" whistled Godfried.

"Say wha'?" questioned Orville.

"Well, Serb—the Jime original—got it. And now I am in control. Guess what I am going to do? I am going to find me Bienfang," Godfried explained with a giddiness Serbinand had not recently heard.

"For realz?" Serbinand and Free squeaked.

"Well, what about us?" Serb asked, sounding confused.

"Who knows?" Godfried paused, "I'm going to take things into my own hands for a bit.... Yes, I'm going to hijack it!"

"Hijack what?" asked Serb. "This story... of course."

~ ~ ~

["*Wait! Stop! Hold up!*," Those were the only words Author attempted to utter. But, they were drowned out by some energy force created by Godfried.]

~ ~ ~

"Okay, Okay, Okay…. I. SAID. OK. Enough!" I spoke. "Who am I? That's so nice of you to ask…and that really isn't important, at least right now. I was brought in to help bring this chapter to a close, so to speak. Someone has to at least put the words down. Otherwise, how can you read them when the story is being hijacked.

To be clear, some time has passed between paragraphs. It's time I fill you in and keep you up to date. And then we can all go on our merry ways.

Serb and Free arrived at the *Schuzzpppluzz Festival* and have been partying there ever since. Back on Earth, after learning that Hawaiian Pizza was a must-have food, Serbinand was determined to experience it. At that same moment, he actually walked past a poster for a bodybuilding contest. The top prize was a trip to *Hawaii*. So, with a destination and goal in mind, Serbinand and Orville took the next steps to learn how to get their body and mind ready for the competition.

Godfried is still on his quest to find Bienfang…and The Author? Well, let's just say, there is nothing he can say."

~ ~ ~

Beeeeeeep… Beeeep Beep.

🎵🎵🎵... tada tada tada dumm... 🎵🎵🎵... 🎵🎵🎵

Will this story continue? What's Bienfang?

Did Godfried actually take over? What did they do to Author?

Is Serbinand really going to get up on stage? Who's writing this?

Those questions and more are answered in the next edition of *The Ridiculous Series*.

"Well... It's actually just *The Ridiculous Adventures of* GODFRIED!"

"No, it's Serbinand's adventures, Jime's adventures too, also Orville!... Yikes...err...oh oh, what is happening?!"

Those questions and more are answered in the next edition of *The Ridiculous: Book 2– Godfried's Turn*.

"That'll do. For now..."

~THE END~

GET TO KNOW THE AUTHORS

JEFFREY NEIL KIPPEL & MINDY HEATHER BLACKSTIEN

For 25 years, Jeff and Mindy have been a powerhouse duo, known to dream big and turn what seems Ridiculous into the remarkable.

The Fitness Revolution Their first Ridiculous venture together wasn't just a project—it was a movement that revolutionized the fitness industry. Through FAME Media Group, they created a network that spanned the globe, featuring fitness events, wellness expos, educational forums, and a talent agency for natural athletes. They published global magazines, produced TV shows across five continents, including a #1 hit on Canada's TSN, and founded the World Natural Sports Organization (WNSO). The FAME World Tour empowered millions to transform their bodies naturally, redefining what it meant to be a bodybuilder—without steroids—at any age, gender, or background.

This movement inspired countless people worldwide to embark on personal transformations. Many became influencers, specialists, and innovators in this growing industry. Even more Ridiculous? Tribes in Africa walked for days to join FAME, and warring nations set aside their differences to promote self-love and fitness.

The Ridiculous Series

Jeff's teenage passion project, *The Ridiculous*, (this very book), seemed Ridiculous to revive—but he did, and decades later, it's a reality. Leveraging Mindy's expertise as an accomplished editor, the series defied outside naysayers, becoming a #1 Amazon bestseller in categories like Happiness, Science Fiction, Comedy, and Self-Help & Psychology Humor.

Now, Jeff and Mindy are collaborating on its trilogy of trilogies, creating a fully immersive 3D metaverse where fans of *The Ridiculous* can interact with the characters or contribute through fan fiction. They are also inviting readers to become part of the journey and the "Dream Big - Do Ridiculous - Achieve Remarkable" campaign, where you may even find yourself mentioned in the story!

Empowerment Space

After years of transforming lives through fitness, Jeff and Mindy realized that looking and performing like a superhero doesn't guarantee happiness. This led them on a decade-long, Ridiculous quest to elevate how people think, function, and feel. They developed a gamified accountability system designed to help anyone achieve their dreams, supported by insights from leaders in mindset, health, and empowerment.

Professional Lives

Jeff and Mindy's journey has been marked by innovation and a relentless pursuit of their passions. Jeff launched the country's first environmental magazine, Recover, while still in university, earning endorsements from Farley Mowat and government officials. Meanwhile, Mindy's childhood passion for wrestling led her to create official fan clubs for her favorite stars, a Ridiculous endeavor that added an entertainment factor to FAME. Both have served on advisory boards, helped companies achieve billion-dollar valuations, and spoken to thousands worldwide through various media. Their influence continues to inspire and empower countless individuals to embrace wellness and pursue their own remarkable goals.

Personal Life

After 25 years together, Jeff and Mindy still find joy in each other's company. They love nature hikes, savoring good food, capturing moments with photography, and dancing at the front of the stage during live music shows. Ridiculously enough, they've taken up learning the keyboard, guitar, and possibly drums, harmonica, and singing. They've also been knighted by archbishops, becoming Sir Jeffrey Neil and Lady Mindy Heather—so feel free to curtsey if you must. They've even been adopted by an Indigenous tribe, officially becoming members of the Taino tribe.

In their latest Ridiculous adventure, they discovered that they're cat people too. Their talkative, fitness-flipping cat, Aura, is the newest addition to the family. If their sweet dogs, Little Dude, Stomp, and Boskoh, were still around, they may have eaten her though!

Their Dream

Mindy and Jeff aspire for *The Ridiculous* to ignite your creativity, turning your Ridiculous ideas into remarkable achievements. Looking for inspiration? Imagine your own take on The Ridiculous characters, scenes, or songs—your creation could find its way into the next book or animated series.

GRATITUDES

Douglas Adams, thank you! You inspired *The Ridiculous* series. After the final *Hitchhiker's Guide to the Galaxy*, teenage Jeff, who loved that style of humor, wanted more. So, he decided to create it.

Since then, we have been mentored by amazing minds, many whose shared wisdom is infused into the pages of *The Ridiculous*. So, while fictional, embedded within our novels are messages about life, the universe and everything—thanks to them!

This Specific Project

We truly appreciate every single person who joined us for our book launch evening full of fun and entertainment. The venue was super cool and featured an 8-piece band (thank you, Trevor Cape & the Field), the characters' favorite space snacks, and an emcee known in the wrestling entertainment world (thanks, Steeephen). But just as we were about to get started…PLOT TWIST. Yes, we were interrupted by a…FIRE! While smoky stairwells, hot walls, and loud alarms derailed the event—and we apologize for the, umm, inconvenience (thankfully, everyone was safe)—it did give us material for future books in the series. Plus, any of you who were there may just find yourselves written in.

Beyond that, it should be known that some (many) of the ridiculous situations shared in the book, actually occurred (well, practically). Meaning they are based on real-life antics of Jeff and his childhood friends—Barry, Dave and Jack (who recently joined the heavenly realms). Thank you to all of you!

A big thanks to Alan Irving, voice actor extraordinaire, whose narration deepened our love for our own characters. He even made us LOL at our own jokes.

Appreciation also goes to Stephanie Wilson for her editing skills and ease of collaboration, and to Samantha M Bailey whose kindness included introducing Stephanie. Then there's RE:becca Eckler for her RE:diculous wisdom and brand-shifting advice.

A special shoutout to Elaine Blackstien, aka Mindy's mom, who made a ridiculous decision to write and publish a book, The Magical Adventures of Lori & Bonnie B. Bunny, at almost 80 years old—how inspiring is she? Very. She's the one who sparked our book-publishing dreams!

Another special mention goes to Jeff's wild and ridiculously cool mom, Rosalie Dinkin, who enthusiastically supports just about everything we do. In fact, it was Rosalie who bought our very first book and audiobook. She'll probably buy this one too! Maybe even turn it into a 1000-piece puzzle, and frame it for her wall.

Remembering our Roots

Our gratitude also extends to each thought leader who guided us along the way in self-discovery, self-expansion, self-care, self-health, and self-love. They may discover that their insights, catch-phrases and noteworthy notes weave their way through the pages of the series:

Casey Combden, a renowned human potentialist, has empowered

hundreds of thousands to dream their dreams and transform their minds. Known by many as The Legend, Casey is a longtime friend of ours. He made us realize that thoughts and emotions are ours to control. Thanks, Casey.

Dave Sandoval, author of the Green Foods Bible, is also a visionary Soulpreneur who has helped millions of people healthify their body through whole food. Thanks, Dave for the quality time at your ranch and the mind-blowing sessions we shared together. Our conversations, and your education, changed how we think about food.

Tony Priddle, once a celebrated NRL rugby league pro footballer, has reinvented himself as a "mind-mechanic." He now leverages his experiences as a top athlete and his passion as a peak performance coach to help others optimize both their sport and their mindset. Thanks, Tony! You've also helped us optimize ourselves and continue to do so. :)

Ian Walling, once a Professional Bodybuilder World Champion and elite-level wholistic trainer, transitioned into roles as a Life Coach, Breathwork Facilitator, Product Innovator, Author, and Retreat Host. These endeavors are fueled by insights gained from his years training as an athlete, acting as an artist sculpting his physique, and serving as a trainer for numerous champions. As one of our closest friends, Ian has taught us a ton! His mind continually amazes us. Thanks Ian.

Dr. Dori, the Birth Doula who inspired the name 'Door' to the Sky of Angels and the character Doc Dor, is a powerhouse: educator, wellness detective, entrepreneur, podcast host, and course leader.

Plus, she had been a wellspring of insights for Mindy, with their talks generally leaving a lasting impact.

(Btw, it's Dr. Dori's healthy living tip that you may find yourself...umm...singing. If you do, tag #DocDor #DoRidiculous #DoRi)

Lisa Borden, the creator of The Wellness Intelligence Collective (TWIC), offers a wealth of information online. It was Lisa who introduced us to the concepts of Wellness Intelligence, Say Yes, Empathy Economics, and Exercise Snacks. Aspects of each have become part of our lives, shaping our thoughts and influencing the series. Thank you, Lisa, for pursuing your purpose with such passion.

Darrell, Sage & Lorie, health intuitives who founded a non-surgical healing modality, also certify people to be trainers in emotional intelligence. Thanks for inviting us to shadow you for the year. We learned a ton. What a phenomenal yet utterly ridiculous adventure. It gave us great memories to use in this story, and even inspired the character The Doc.

Bharangi, who owns and operates The Rising Sun sanctuary, is also a metaphysical mentor and spiritual teacher. Her kindness and insights were key to our journey. Plus she ordained us as metaphysical ministers. Thanks Bharangi!

Dr. Ben, who is well-connected in the political world, coordinated our adoption into the Taino Tribe and arranged for us to be knighted by archbishops. Thank you so much for the ceremony and ridiculous experiences. One of our life's most memorable.

To the late Brian Gangel, chairman of the World Organization of

Natural Medicine, we thank you for taking us under your wings, educating us on so much, and believing in our vision.

Very happy to have been able to honor the memory of our brother-in-law Mohx, his wife Wobeen (our sis), and their kids Cheez and Ron-T by including their coined term "snackventure" into the story. It fits so well!

Of course, much love to the rest of our families: nephews, nieces, siblings (and siblings-in-law), our moms, and both our dads (RIP). We thought of you when we imagined people reading our stories. We hope you love what our imaginations created as much as we enjoyed imagining it!

Each Other

We are both thrilled to have come together to co-create on yet another project. Our resulting growth, magical moments, and shared experiences are awesome chapters in our life adventure.

- To Mindy (with love from Jeff): I want to express my deepest, most sincere gratitude to you, and for you. Thank you for elevating my story to an entirely new level. I truly appreciate you inspiring me to pursue my passion and being my unwavering cheerleader throughout the years. You mean the world to me... Thank you, thank you, thank you!
- To Jeff (with love from Mindy): I still remember how proud you were when you first told me about this project. It was on our first date, lol. Who knew I would become such a big part of it? I am happy we decided to pool our

resources in this venture and in life too. It has also been fun entering your ridiculous imagination and learning more about how your mind works. Thank you!

Finally, thank you to you, our readers. We appreciate you dearly for focusing on our words. Hope our imagination made you laugh, rethink or get inspired. If you do happen to take action on your own ridiculous pursuit, let us know. Share your breakthroughs and triumphs! You can earn rewards, and your stories can even be featured in the Do Ridiculous—Achieve Remarkable spin-off series. How cool is that?!

www.DoRidiculous.com #DoRidiculus

Printed in Great Britain
by Amazon